GCSE English
FOR OCR

JOHN REYNOLDS ★ RON NORMAN

Heinemann

Heinemann is an imprint of Pearson Education Limited,
a company incorporated in England and Wales, having
its registered office at Edinburgh Gate, Harlow, Essex, CM20 2JE.
Registered company number: 872828

Heinemann is a registered trademark of Pearson Education Limited

First published 2002
10 09
10 9

ISBN: 978 0 435 10973 8

Designed and produced by Gecko Ltd, Bicester, Oxon
Printed in China (CTPS/09)

Acknowledgements

The publishers gratefully acknowledge the following for permission to reproduce copyright material. Whilst every effort has been made to trace the copyright holders, in some cases this has proved unsuccessful. The publishers apologise for any omission of original sources and will be pleased to make the necessary arrangements at the first opportunity.

'Malaysia facts' found at www.cia.gov/cia/publications/factbook/geos/my.html: reprinted with the kind permission of Central Intelligence Agency, Washington (CIA). 'Teenage smoking rates fall again' and 'Smoking statistics' from www.ash.org.uk: reprinted with kind permission of ASH. 'Please sponsor a child today' produced by Actionaid: reprinted with the kind permission of Actionaid. 'Boarding' Mizz investigates, from MIZZ magazine, page 26, 3rd April, 2002; copyright © Mizz/Teena Taylor/IPC Syndication: reprinted by permission of IPC Syndications. Extract from Using Cognitive Methods in the Classroom by A. Ashman and R. Conway, published by Routledge in 1993: reprinted by permission of ITPS/Taylor & Francis. 'Cauliflower cheese and mustard soup' by Nigel Slater, from Real Food, published by Fourth Estate in 1998; copyright © Nigel Slater: reprinted by permission of HarperCollins Publishers Limited. Volvo advert and 'Technical specifications'; reproduced with kind permission of Volvo and JJ Marketing. Barnardos advertisements: reprinted with the kind permission of Barnardos. India Tourist office advertisement: reprinted with the kind permission of The India Tourist Office. Orlando brochure page, from 'Thomson Cities and Short Breaks': reprinted with the kind permission of Thomson Breakaway. 'On The Road' by Isabel Lloyd and James Ruppert, from Total Guide: Knowing Your Rights produced for W H Smith: copyright © Isabel Lloyd and James Ruppert: reprinted with the kind permission of the authors. 'Result' by Hugh Wilson, from Total Guide: You and Your Teenager produced for W H Smith; copyright © Hugh Wilson. 'How to use ...... a taxi' by Guy Browning (illustration by Gary Kempston), Guardian Weekend, April 20, 2002; text copyright © The Guardian, illustration copyright © Gary Kempston: text reprinted with the kind permission of The Guardian, illustration reprinted with the kind permission of the illustrator. Extract from Germany edition 1, Lonely Planet, pages 84-85: reprinted by permission of Lonely Planet Publications. 'Why your make-up bag may be making you ill' by Alice Fowler, in The Daily Mail, 23rd April, 2002: reprinted by permission of Atlantic Syndication on behalf of The Daily Mail. 'Walt Disney Studios, Paris' by Andrew Eames, from The Times, 23rd March, 2002; copyright © Andrew Eames/Times Newspapers Limited, London: used with permission. 'Walt Disney Studios, Paris' Disney. Extract from On The Black Hill by Bruce Chatwin, published by Jonathan Cape: used by permission of The Random House Group Limited. Extract from Pentax ME Super Book of Photography by MacDonald, Honeyman and Hornak, published by Hamlyn 1982. Extract from Down the Mine by George Orwell; copyright © George Orwell: reproduced by permission of A. M. Heath & Co. Ltd., on behalf of Mark Hamilton as the Literary Executor of the Estate of the Late Sonia Brownell Orwell, and Martin Secker & Warburg Limited. Extract from Neither Here Nor There by Bill Bryson; copyright © Bill Bryson; published by Black Swan, a division of Transworld Publishers, all rights reserved: used with permission. Extract from My Family and Other Animals by Gerald Durrell; copyright © Gerald Durrell 1956: reproduced with permission of Curtis Brown Limited, London on behalf of The Estate of Gerald Durrell. Extract from A Cab At The Door by V. S. Pritchett, published by Chatto & Windus: used by permission of The Random House Group Limited. 'Industry Targets The Young' from Alcohol Alert Issue 1, 2001: reprinted with permission. 'A Laugh' 'Advice for Young People about Alcohol' booklet published by the Health Education Authority; © Crown Copyright. 'When choice becomes just a memory' by Naomi Klein, from The Guardian, 21 June, 2001; copyright © Naomi Klein, 2001; reprinted by permission of Klein Lewis Productions Limited. Extracts from www.foe.co.uk reprinted with the kind permission of Friends of the Earth. Extract from 'Snapshots of a Wedding' from The Collector of Treasures by Bessie Head, published by Heinemann: reprinted by permission of Heinemann Educational. Extract from 'Two Kinds' by Amy Tan from The Joy Luck Club © 1989 Amy Tan: reprinted by permission of Abner Stein. Extract from 'The Red Bull' by Ismith Khan, from A Day in the Country by Ismith Khan, published by Peepal Tree Press, 1994: reprinted by permission of the publishers. Extract from 'Leela's Friend' by R. K. Narayan, from Malguidi Days first published in Great Britain by William Heinemann in 1982; copyright © 1972, 1975, 1978, 1980, 1981, 1982 by R. K. Narayan: reprinted by permission of Sheil Land Associates Limited. Extract from 'Games at Twilight' by Anita Desai, from Games At Twilight first published by Vintage; copyright © Anita Desai 1978: reproduced by permission of Rogers Coleridge & White Limited, 20 Powis Mews, London W11 1JN. Extract from 'The Tall woman and her Short Husband' by Feng Ji-Cai, translated to English by Gladys Yang © English Translation Gladys Young: reprinted by permission of Yang Zhi (daughter of Gladys Young). Extract from 'The Gold-Legged Frog' translated by Domern Garden, from The Politician and Other Stories published by Silkworm Books: reprinted by permission of the author and Silkworm Books. Review of 'Obi-Wan Computer Game' from Games Master, March, 2002: reprinted with the kind permission of Future Publishing. Review of 'Lord of the Rings' by Colin Kennedy, January, 2001 from www.empireonline.co.uk: reprinted with the kind permission of Colin Kennedy. Comment section by Colin Mitchell, editor, Shoot Monthly, March 2002; copyright © Colin Mitchell/Shoot Monthly/IPC: reprinted by permission of IPC Syndication. 'Should parents be allowed to smack?' by Laura Barton, The Guardian, 3 March, 2002; copyright © Laura Barton, 2002: used with permission. 'Safe Internet Shopping' © Crown Copyright. Social Services Complaints and Compliments leaflet and photo: reproduced with the kind permission of Calderdale Council. 'MMR The facts' © Crown Copyright. 'Motorists are being milked' Daily Express Editorial 5th March, 2002; copyright © Express Newspapers: used with permission. Saab advert reproduced with the kind permission of Saab UK. Extract from Compassion in World Farming – BSE, Salmonella, E Coli, River Pollution, Greenhouse Gases, Animal Suffering – What's the connection? Produced with CIWF: reprinted with permission. Extract from 'Welcome to Barrow in Furness' leaflet; copyright © Barrow Borough Council: used with permission. Extract from Five Acre Virgin by Elizabeth Jolley, published by Fremantle Arts Centre Press: reprinted by permission of David Higham Associates Limited. Extract from The Amber Spyglass by Philip Pullman; copyright © Philip Pullman, 2000 the third and final book in the His Dark Materials trilogy, published by Scholastic Children's Books, all rights reserved: reproduced by permission of Scholastic Limited. Extract from My Left Foot by Christy Brown, published by Secker & Warburg: used by permission of The Random House Group Limited. Extract from The Fellowship of the Ring by J R R Tolkien: reprinted by permission of HarperCollins Publishers Limited. 'You're' from Collected Poems by Sylvia Plath, published by Faber and Faber Limited: reprinted by permission of Faber and Faber Limited

Copyright permissions sought by Jackie Newman

Original illustrations @ Heinemann Educational Publishers 2002
Illustrations: Yane Christensen, Alice Englander, Teressa Flavin, Gecko Ltd, Rosalind Hudson, Karin Littlewood, Georgina McBain, Kathryn Prewett, Nick Schon, John Storey, Jennifer Ward, Martin Ursell

The Publishers would like to thank the following for permission to reproduce photographs on the pages noted: Actionplus, pp50, 142; Alamy, p15; Barrow Museum Service, p102; Gareth Boden, pp25, 26; Collections/Ashley Cooper, p102; Corbis, pp94, 96, 103; Corbis/Bettmann, p144; Corbis/Nick Wheeler, p126; Empics/Barry Coombs, p84; Friends of the Earth/Nick Cobbing, pp58, 59; IPC Syndication/Teena Taylor, p18; The Kobal Collection, p126; PA Photos, pp18, 85, 101; Pentax, p41; Robert Harding Picture Library, pp51, 63; The Ronald Grant Archive, pp124, 131; Travel Ink/Andrew Cowin, p38; John Walmsley, pp12, 28-30, 33

CONTENTS

Unit 3/4   Literary heritage and imaginative writing   113

Why English matters

When you begin your course in GCSE English, you are already something of an expert in the language. After all, you use it every day to communicate in a variety of situations in both speech and writing. If English is your mother tongue, you have been learning the language since you were a baby and using it with increasing sophistication all the time since then.

These are just some of the things you have already learned:

- You can recognise and say the sounds of English.
- You have built up a large working vocabulary of English words.
- You know how to put words together in different kinds and lengths of sentences.
- You have begun to learn how to vary the style of language you use according to the situation you are in.
- You have learned how to produce writing in different forms and for different purposes.
- You have been learning how to spell and punctuate your writing accurately.

Your GCSE English course builds on all of this previous learning – and is designed to help you develop your English language skills even further, so that by the time you complete the course, you can use English effectively and accurately in a wide range of situations in life, at work or in further education.

There are many reasons why it is important for you to develop your English skills. Consider some of the suggestions in the table below.

1 Decide for yourself as an individual which are the most and least important reasons. Rank these from 1 (the *most* important) to 7 (*least* important).

2 In groups of three or four, compare your rankings, and through discussion, try to agree on a group ranking.

Why does English matter?	My ranking	Group ranking
Improving my English skills will help me in other subjects.		
Language is power: better language skills give me more power in my life.		
It is fun to learn more about the language we use.		
Improving my English will give me more confidence.		
Being able to understand different kinds of writing puts me in touch with new ideas.		
I enjoy reading stories, poems and plays. They make me think.		
I need a good grade to progress to the next stage of my education or get a job.		

How to use this book

The student

This book is organised in accordance with the different parts of the OCR GCSE English examination. It introduces you to the basic requirements of the exam, a variety of texts that are typical of the material you have to study, and plenty of practice activities.

You may find it easiest to follow the different sections in the book in order, though it may well be that you are studying these with your teacher in a different sequence or even studying two or more parts at the same time.

As you work through the book you will find:

- information and guidance about the skills you will be tested on in the GCSE exam
- texts and activities to enable you to practise your skills
- important points to remember about the use of English
- special technical terms
- tips for success from an examiner.

Health Warning: Reading is good for you

The key to success in English can be summed up in one word: **reading**.
No single textbook can be a substitute for your own reading. Make reading your habit – newspapers, magazines, fiction and non-fiction books, information on the Internet – and your own command of English will keep on growing.

The teacher

Although the book is organised according to Units 1–4 of the OCR specification, not all teachers will wish to tackle these sequentially, and it is certainly not our assumption that they will do so. There are also many opportunities for using the material in the reading sections as the stimulus for writing (and speaking and listening) activities.

In Units 2 and 3/4, most of the text extracts have been drawn from the OCR anthologies (*Opening Lines* and *Opening Worlds*) and one of the Shakespeare plays specified for the examined option (*Much Ado About Nothing*) but we hope that the kinds of approach and activities suggested here might be equally applicable to alternative texts. We also hope that the material in Unit 3/4 will be equally useful in preparing students for either the coursework or examination option.

Throughout the book, icons and colour coding have been used to identify activities and material of different kinds as shown below. Important technical terms are set in bold the first time they appear and are explained in the glossary of Key Terms on page 160.

 assessment objectives

 audience, purpose, technique

 suggested coursework activity

 opportunity to research on the Internet

 opportunity for the development of specific literacy elements

 opportunity for the development and assessment of speaking and listening activities

 opportunity for the development and assessment of writing activities

Your skills in English

Improving your reading skills

The biggest single step you can take towards improving your reading skills is to set aside some time each day to read a little of what you fancy. Start to look at some of this material critically, noticing how different styles of language are used according to the purpose of the text, the place it appears and the people it is written for.

On your GCSE course, you will read many different kinds of texts. These will include:

- ✓ informative non-fiction texts
- ✓ texts produced in a number of different media (newspapers, magazines, etc.)
- ✓ texts that try to persuade or influence you (adverts, articles, speeches)
- ✓ fictional texts, such as short stories, including those written by writers from different cultures
- ✓ poetry, both ancient and modern
- ✓ drama, including a play by Shakespeare.

As you practise your reading, you will:

- ✓ become familiar with the style and formats of different kinds of text
- ✓ learn different ways of reading different texts – for example, we read poems differently from the way we read adverts
- ✓ learn to distinguish between facts and opinions
- ✓ learn to 'read between the lines'
- ✓ continue to expand your vocabulary
- ✓ recognise and comment on the different ways in which writers organise and structure their texts
- ✓ recognise and comment on the ways that writers use language to achieve their effects.

Improving your writing skills

As with reading, there is only one effective way of improving your writing skills – that is, by doing lots of it.

On your GCSE course, you will practise many different kinds of writing. These include writing that is designed to:

- ✓ inform, explain and describe
- ✓ analyse, review and comment
- ✓ argue, persuade and advise
- ✓ explore, imagine and entertain.

One way of thinking about the differences between types of writing is to consider the reason, or **purpose**, behind a text. Good writers also think about whom they are writing for – their **audience** – and choose their words very carefully so they achieve just the right style. Good writing also requires careful **planning** – and you may often need to draft and re-draft a piece of writing before getting it just right.

Therefore in all your writing, remember to take care to:

✓ use correct spelling   ✓ use correct punctuation
✓ separate sentences by using full stops appropriately
✓ use correct grammatical expression
✓ organise your ideas into well-structured paragraphs
✓ write legibly and present your work neatly.

However, bear in mind that the best grades are achieved by those students who can write with some *style*. This means:

✓ writing in an appropriate tone and register
✓ choosing vocabulary carefully to convey the precise meaning of what you intend to say and not just using the first word that comes into your head
✓ varying the length and type of sentences in order to involve and interest the reader
✓ structuring your writing logically to build to a planned and forceful conclusion.

Improving your speaking and listening

Although most of this book is given over to the development of your reading and writing skills, we hope that the various activities suggested will allow you to continue to develop your oral skills in English.

Your teacher will need to assess your speaking and listening work in three different contexts:

✓ taking part in a group discussion activity
✓ making a more extended individual contribution (such as a talk you have prepared)
✓ taking part in a drama-type activity (such as a role play).

As with reading and writing, good speaking and listening involves 'tuning in' to the right style of language that is appropriate to the situation you are in. This means:

✓ talking clearly and using appropriate vocabulary
✓ using the correct forms of standard English, especially in more formal situations
✓ listening and responding to other people
✓ using language effectively to convey your ideas or feelings.

Finally, we hope that you find your English course interesting and satisfying.
Good luck with your studies and, of course, with the exam!

Non-fiction, media and information

UNIT 1

In this part of your course, and in the examination that you take, you will develop and demonstrate your **reading** skills (Section A) and **writing** skills (Section B).

Section A requires you to produce *two* pieces of writing, one each based on your study of:

- an unseen non-fiction text or texts
- an unseen media and information text or texts.

You may be asked to provide information from more than one text.

Each of these is worth 10% of the total marks for English.

Section B requires you to produce *one* piece of writing that is designed to **inform**, **explain** and/or **describe**. The task will be broadly linked to the reading material in Section A.

This is also worth 10% of the total marks for English.

The particular skills (**Assessment objectives**) involved in this Unit are listed below.

In **Section A** you will need to:

- ✔ distinguish between fact and opinion
- ✔ follow an argument
- ✔ select and collate material
- ✔ understand and evaluate a writer's techniques.

In **Section B** you will need to:

- ✔ write clearly and imaginatively
- ✔ use language suitable for different readers and purposes
- ✔ organise your writing into sentences, paragraphs and whole texts
- ✔ use different kinds of sentences to achieve particular effects
- ✔ spell and punctuate your work accurately.

Reading non-fiction, media and information texts

Remember that you are going to read two different types of text: **non-fiction** and **media and information**. (We will refer to the latter as media texts from now on.) So, what is the difference between them?

Non-fiction texts are generally factual and they are written to inform, explain and describe. Examples include instruction leaflets or manuals on how to do something (such as use a mobile phone, repair a car, use a personal computer). A recipe is another example of an instruction text. They contain facts rather than opinions.

Media texts are generally more persuasive and have a specific audience in mind. They are more emotive and biased towards the information they present. Examples include advertisements to persuade you to buy particular products, opinion columns in newspapers and magazines, and pamphlets to persuade you to support charities. Thus they will contain both opinions and facts. Take care – sometimes opinions are cleverly disguised as facts!

How to distinguish between non-fiction and media texts

 **ACTIVITY 1**

Working in groups, look at Texts 1 and 2 below.

1 Decide which is non-fiction and which is a media text.

2 Explain your decisions to the rest of the class.

Text 1

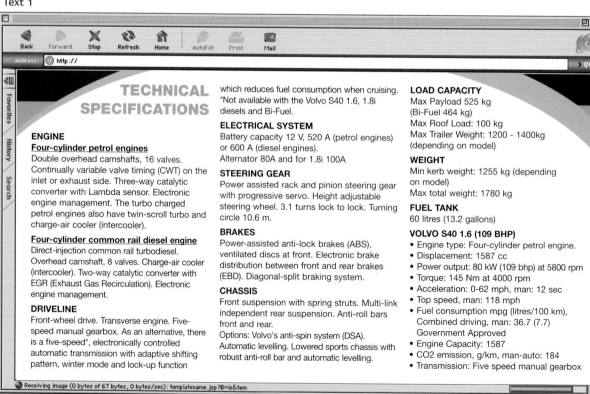

TECHNICAL SPECIFICATIONS

ENGINE

Four-cylinder petrol engines
Double overhead camshafts, 16 valves. Continually variable valve timing (CWT) on the inlet or exhaust side. Three-way catalytic converter with Lambda sensor. Electronic engine management. The turbo charged petrol engines also have twin-scroll turbo and charge-air cooler (intercooler).

Four-cylinder common rail diesel engine
Direct-injection common rail turbodiesel. Overhead camshaft, 8 valves. Charge-air cooler (intercooler). Two-way catalytic converter with EGR (Exhaust Gas Recirculation). Electronic engine management.

DRIVELINE
Front-wheel drive. Transverse engine. Five-speed manual gearbox. As an alternative, there is a five-speed*, electronically controlled automatic transmission with adaptive shifting pattern, winter mode and lock-up function

which reduces fuel consumption when cruising. *Not available with the Volvo S40 1.6, 1.8i diesels and Bi-Fuel.

ELECTRICAL SYSTEM
Battery capacity 12 V, 520 A (petrol engines) or 600 A (diesel engines). Alternator 80A and for 1.8i 100A

STEERING GEAR
Power assisted rack and pinion steering gear with progressive servo. Height adjustable steering wheel. 3.1 turns lock to lock. Turning circle 10.6 m.

BRAKES
Power-assisted anti-lock brakes (ABS), ventilated discs at front. Electronic brake distribution between front and rear brakes (EBD). Diagonal-split braking system.

CHASSIS
Front suspension with spring struts. Multi-link independent rear suspension. Anti-roll bars front and rear.
Options: Volvo's anti-spin system (DSA). Automatic levelling. Lowered sports chassis with robust anti-roll bar and automatic levelling.

LOAD CAPACITY
Max Payload 525 kg
(Bi-Fuel 464 kg)
Max Roof Load: 100 kg
Max Trailer Weight: 1200 - 1400kg
(depending on model)

WEIGHT
Min kerb weight: 1255 kg (depending on model)
Max total weight: 1780 kg

FUEL TANK
60 litres (13.2 gallons)

VOLVO S40 1.6 (109 BHP)
• Engine type: Four-cylinder petrol engine.
• Displacement: 1587 cc
• Power output: 80 kW (109 bhp) at 5800 rpm
• Torque: 145 Nm at 4000 rpm
• Acceleration: 0-62 mph, man: 12 sec
• Top speed, man: 118 mph
• Fuel consumption mpg (litres/100 km), Combined driving, man: 36.7 (7.7) Government Approved
• Engine Capacity: 1587
• CO2 emission, g/km, man-auto: 184
• Transmission: Five speed manual gearbox

Back Forward Stop Refresh Home AutoFill Print Mail

Address: http://   go

Favorites History Search

Receiving image (0 bytes of 67 bytes, 0 bytes/sec): templatename.jsp?B=ie&tem

Text 2

You probably correctly identified that Text 2 is a media text. It does tell you some facts about the car but its main purpose is to persuade you to buy it. It does this in two different ways: visually and through the vocabulary. It clearly has a specific audience in mind.

Text 1 is an example of a non-fiction text; it explains the facts only, namely the technical specifications.

Audience and purpose

An easy way to work out the difference between non-fiction texts and media texts is to ask yourself the following three questions.

- Who is the intended audience?
- What is the purpose?
- What techniques does the writer use?

You can easily remember the questions by remembering the mnemonic APT (audience, purpose, technique).

Distinguish between fact and opinion

Look at the texts below.

Text 1

> The detached house comprises two living rooms, a kitchen and a utility room on the ground floor. Upstairs are three bedrooms, and a bathroom. There is a south-facing garden at the rear of the property covering an area of 30 square metres.

Text 2

> Your dream house. Rooms on the ground floor are ideally designed to provide comfort and luxury. The bedrooms are peaceful and all look out on to the exciting scenery of the town centre. The garden, with its state-of-the-art water feature, is a haven of peace and tranquillity.

Do these texts describe the same house? Quite possibly they might, but they take a very different approach to doing so. Text 1 contains **facts**. It tells us the number and type of rooms on both floors of the house, the size of the garden and the position of it. Text 2 uses the same facts – it even includes a couple more (what are they?) but it relies much more on presenting **opinions** that are implied by the writer's choice of words.

ACTIVITY 2

1 List the facts that you have learned about the house from the two texts above.

2 From Text 2, list what you consider to be the writer's opinions about the house and the words that convey those opinions.

3 Try substituting the writer's words with words of opposite meaning and consider the effects you can produce.

ACTIVITY 3

Now look at the following statements.

> Sir Steven Redgrave is the greatest sportsman ever.

1 Which of these statements are facts and which are opinions?

> The first animal to be cloned was a sheep called Dolly.

> **Sir Steven Redgrave has won five Olympic gold medals.**

> **Chips are disgusting and eating them makes you fat.**

> Chips are made out of potatoes.   *CLONING ANIMALS IS WRONG.*

2 How did you decide?

3 How do the dictionary definitions below help you to decide which of the statements above are facts and which are opinions? What about the last statement?

> **Fact**, n. thing that is (known to be) true.   **Opinion**, n. belief based on grounds short of proof, view held as probably, what one thinks about something.

Context

It is important to keep in your mind the **context** in which a statement is made when you are judging whether it is factual or not. You need to consider what else was being talked about at the time, the person who made the statement, and the person(s) being spoken to.

ACTIVITY 4

1 How would you respond to the statement on the right about chips if it were made to you by:

> Chips are disgusting and eating them makes you fat.

  ● your best friend when you were buying lunch in the school canteen?

  ● a doctor talking to your Year group as part of your school's healthy eating week?

2 Can you think of ways to rephrase the statement to turn it into a fact?

Whoever says it, the first three words of the statement are certainly an opinion; the word 'disgusting' conveys that. However, what about the rest of the sentence? If it's said by your friend in the context of the dinner queue, your response might well be, 'Go on, then. Prove it!' Would you say the same to the doctor? You'd be more likely to believe the statement in the context of a health talk, but, as it stands, it still remains an opinion.

 REMEMBER

A skilled writer knows that it is not difficult to disguise opinions as facts.

A skilled reader is someone who is not fooled by this approach.

Often, media texts in particular present opinions and make them sound like facts. The following simple test will help you identify which is which. Try putting the following phrases in front of any statement:

✦ The writer *knows* that ...   ✦ The writer *thinks* that ...

If you can add the first then you are looking at a fact. If you can add the second, you are reading an opinion. Test this out with the description of the house on page 12.

Words, words, words

The words that writers choose and their associations can influence your response to a text.

 ## ACTIVITY 5

Look again at Text 2 on page 12 and consider the use of the words:

◆ dream   ◆ comfort   ◆ luxury   ◆ exciting   ◆ haven.

1 Why do you think these words were used to describe the house?

2 What are their associations?

3 Do they convey facts or opinions?

Presenting objective facts

ACTIVITY 6

Look at the following details about the country of Malaysia.

1 What comments can you make about the way they have been presented?

2 Who do you think would be likely to want to use them?

3 How much use would they be to someone who was planning a holiday in the country?

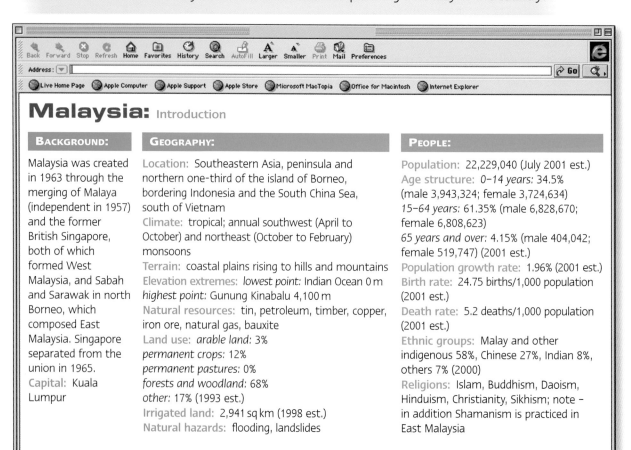

Malaysia: Introduction

BACKGROUND:

Malaysia was created in 1963 through the merging of Malaya (independent in 1957) and the former British Singapore, both of which formed West Malaysia, and Sabah and Sarawak in north Borneo, which composed East Malaysia. Singapore separated from the union in 1965.
Capital: Kuala Lumpur

GEOGRAPHY:

Location: Southeastern Asia, peninsula and northern one-third of the island of Borneo, bordering Indonesia and the South China Sea, south of Vietnam
Climate: tropical; annual southwest (April to October) and northeast (October to February) monsoons
Terrain: coastal plains rising to hills and mountains
Elevation extremes: *lowest point:* Indian Ocean 0 m *highest point:* Gunung Kinabalu 4,100 m
Natural resources: tin, petroleum, timber, copper, iron ore, natural gas, bauxite
Land use: *arable land:* 3%
permanent crops: 12%
permanent pastures: 0%
forests and woodland: 68%
other: 17% (1993 est.)
Irrigated land: 2,941 sq km (1998 est.)
Natural hazards: flooding, landslides

PEOPLE:

Population: 22,229,040 (July 2001 est.)
Age structure: *0–14 years:* 34.5% (male 3,943,324; female 3,724,634)
15–64 years: 61.35% (male 6,828,670; female 6,808,623)
65 years and over: 4.15% (male 404,042; female 519,747) (2001 est.)
Population growth rate: 1.96% (2001 est.)
Birth rate: 24.75 births/1,000 population (2001 est.)
Death rate: 5.2 deaths/1,000 population (2001 est.)
Ethnic groups: Malay and other indigenous 58%, Chinese 27%, Indian 8%, others 7% (2000)
Religions: Islam, Buddhism, Daoism, Hinduism, Christianity, Sikhism; note – in addition Shamanism is practiced in East Malaysia

From the CIA website

These details are nothing more than **objective facts**. This means their accuracy can be checked very easily by anyone who is prepared to do so.

However, what about the information contained in the following material?

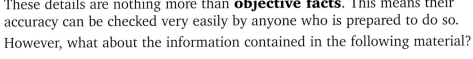

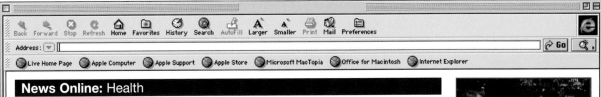

News Online: Health

Teenage smoking rates fall again

Smoking among teenagers has fallen again in the past year – but official figures show levels of drug use are up.

An Office of National Statistics (ONS) survey of schoolchildren aged between 11 and 15 showed 9% smoked regularly in the past 12 months, compared to 11% the previous year.

The 9% figure was significantly down on the 13% of young people who smoked regularly according to a similar survey in 1996, suggesting the decline is real.

But 12% had used drugs in the past year – slightly up from the figure of 11% for 1998.

Meanwhile, following a fall in the proportion of pupils who drank alcohol between 1996 and 1998, there was no further change in the past year.

The ONS interviewed more than 9,000 pupils in 340 schools across England about their drug use, and smoking and drinking habits in the autumn of 1999.

More girls smoke than boys, with 10% of teenage girls having at least one cigarette a week, compared to 8% of their male classmates.

And while only 1% of 11-year-olds smoke, almost a quarter of 15-year-olds regularly have a cigarette.

But health ministers welcomed the drop, which comes on World No Tobacco Day and after the government has pledged to reduce the number of smokers by 1.5 million over the next decade.

Target

The target includes a pledge to reduce the rate of all teenage smoking to 11% by 2005 and to 9% by 2010.

Although today's statistics show that figure has already been achieved with young teenagers, up to 40% of older teenagers still smoke.

A spokesman for the Department of Health said: 'These figures show that the smoking rates are heading in the right direction, but we know we can't be complacent about this.

'We need to continue with health prevention measures and enforcement of the law to make sure young teenagers cannot buy cigarettes.'

Amanda Sandford at Action on Smoking and Health, said: 'It is very good news. I think it would be fair to assume this is the beginning of a downward trend.

'All credit to the government – their policies are paying off.

The figures for drug use also showed differences by age, with just 1% of 11-year-olds using illegal substances in the last year, compared to a third of 15-year-olds.

Cannabis was most likely to be used, with 11% of pupils admitting to taking the drug in the last year.

The next most commonly used substances – glue, gas and 'poppers' – had only been used by 2% of youngsters.

And more than a third of all the pupils and 62% of 15-year-olds said they had been offered drugs.

One in five of the pupils said they had had an alcoholic drink in the last week, unchanged from 1999.

These figures show that the smoking rates are heading in the right direction, but we know we can't be complacent
Department of Health

Regular teenage smokers

1996 – 13%
1998 – 11%
1999 – 9%

Smoking statistics

Percentage of school pupils who are regular smokers, England

	Age 11–16		
	Boys	**Girls**	**All**
1982	11	11	11
1984	13	13	13
1986	7	12	10
1988	7	9	8
1990	9	11	10
1992	9	10	10
1994	10	13	12
1996	11	15	13
1998	9	12	11
1999	8	10	9
2000	9	12	10
2001	8	11	10

'The key thing now is to get rid of tobacco promotion and look at keeping up the health promotion message.'

Government targets

The target is to reduce smoking among 11–15 year olds from 13% in 1996 to 11% in 2005 and 9% by 2010. The target for 2010 has already been reached (if teenage smoking does not rise again).

ACTIVITY 7

The information on page 15 is taken from a BBC web page about teenage smoking and drug use. Read the text carefully. In note form write down the **facts** you have found out about:

- the smoking habits of children aged 11–15
- the difference in the smoking habits of boys and girls
- the smoking habits of 15-year-olds between 1982 and 2001
- teenagers' use of alcohol and drugs.

You have identified facts, but, remember, you can still interpret and present them in different ways depending on your personal point of view.

 ## ACTIVITY 8

Write one paragraph for each of the following headlines. By paying careful attention to your choice of vocabulary and the tone of voice in which you address your readers you should be able to present the facts you've identified for opposing purposes.

Fall in teenage smoking gives encouraging signals

One in ten teenagers experiments with drinks, drugs and alcohol

Presentation and interpretation

Look at the leaflet for ActionAid opposite. You will notice that this sets out to catch the reader's attention not just by words, but by the ways in which the words are presented on the page. There are photographs, sub-headings, different colours, quotations, bold and italic type and the organisation's logo printed in the bottom right-hand corner. All of these are known as **presentational devices** and are important means by which writers involve and interest their readers.

 ## ACTIVITY 9

On pages 18–19 you will find some examples of non-fiction and media texts. Working in pairs, analyse Texts 1 to 3 and answer the following questions on each text.

- Is it a media or non-fiction text?
- Who is the intended audience?
- What is its purpose?
- What techniques does the writer use?
- Does it contain facts, opinions or a mixture of both?

Support your answers with examples from the text.

Because you care about
the child who is suffering

Sponsor a child today and help change their life forever

'When ActionAid started working in my village, things started to change. ActionAid helped us build a school. Me and my friends have started going to school for the first time. We are learning lots of things that we will need when we are older. I am very happy because it means we will have a better future.'

Saibu, Ghana

Your sponsorship can make a world of difference

A child who doesn't have enough food to eat, who has nothing other than dirty water to drink, who lacks healthcare and can only dream about going to school faces a future of extreme poverty where they will struggle to survive.

A child like this needs help – your help. And through child sponsorship, which costs only 50p a day, you can change their life. You can help give them, and their community, the chance of a real future free from poverty. And you'll receive letters, drawings and other feedback from the child you sponsor – so you can see for yourself just what a difference your support has made.

Please return the form today.

Every day, 35,000 children die of hunger-related causes.

Because you care about
the child who is hungry

Children living in poor communities often come from families that go to bed hungry every night – simply because they cannot grow enough food to feed themselves. Poor people often struggle to farm dry and infertile soil without adequate tools or fertilisers.

Because you care about
the child who can't read or write

More than 113 million children don't have access to primary education.

Children who have been denied their education – either because they have to work or because there is no school in their area – have little chance of escaping the poverty that they were born into.

Yet sponsorship will help a child go to school and learn the vital skills that they need to secure reliable livelihoods for themselves. It will also help us set up adult literacy classes – so the whole community will have the knowledge they need to take control of their lives.

Please sponsor a child today

More than 3 million people, most of whom are children die from diarrhoea each year.

Because you care about
the child who is sick

In the world's poorest communities, simple illnesses such as diarrhoea can kill. Without adequate healthcare, poor children continue to suffer and die for the want of medicines that cost just a few pounds.

Child sponsorship means we can ensure a child and their community has a safe, clean supply of water. And it also means we can help them gain access to the healthcare that could save their lives.

Because you care about
the child's whole community

We know from successfully working with poor people for over 30 years that the best way to help a child is to help their community. So when you sponsor a child through ActionAid, you won't just change the life of one child. You'll help their whole community build a future for themselves.

Just £15 a month – that's only 50p a day – is enough to sponsor a child. And as you receive letters and reports over the months, you'll be able to see what an incredible difference you're making to the lives of everyone in their community.

50p a day can change the life of a child and their community.

act!onaid

Somewhere in the world, a child is waiting for your support.

Text 1

(m) investigates

Boarding school

If you think your school day's way too long, what about the people who live there 24/7? mizz brushes up on boarding ...

We all know Will Young's a talented, gorgeous superstar. But did you also know he went to boarding school? Yep, from the age of eight, little Will and twin brother Rupert were shipped off to board at Horris Hill Prep School in Berkshire. Eight's pretty young to be parted from your parents but, hey, it doesn't look like it's done him any harm! And seeing as the numbers of people going to boarding schools have stopped going down this year – for the first time in 20 years – it looks like loads of parents out there are thinking the same thing. According to the Boarding Schools' Association, about 70,000 boys and girls are currently boarding in Britain.

Why board?

Loadsa parents will shiver at the thought of boarding schools – what's the point of having kids if you're just gonna pay someone else to look after them? It ain't as simple as that, though. For some families, going to boarding school's a tradition, but for others it really is the best option. Some parents live overseas, or have demanding jobs that mean they're away a lot. Others have split with their partner and can't juggle everything at once. While for some, it might even be as simple as having no decent schools near their house.

Whatever the reasons, it doesn't make your folks bad parents or mean that they don't care about you. Today's boarding schools are tuned into pupils' feelings but they're not there to provide you with love – you've still got your family for that.

Setting the standards

If you imagine boarding schools as having iron beds, cold showers and a bit of bread for brekkie, think again. Most schools these days are modern and cosy – a real home away from home. But to ensure every school's up to scratch, a new set of guidelines are being published this month, called *The National Boarding Standards*. It insists on stuff like how pupils must be able to personalise their rooms with posters, have space for nick-nacks and be able to phone home in private. If you wanna check these guidelines out, click on to www.boarding.org.uk

Adding it up

Every school's different, but full-time boarding costs, on average, £4,736 per term. Eek! But some schools do offer scholarships to help parents with fees. The Ministry Of Defence also gives an allowance to children whose parents are in the armed forces. Plus, there are 36 state schools in England that accept boarders. These can cost under £2,000 a term.

So what's boarding school like? **mizz** gets the goss from two readers who board at Farringtons and Stratford House in Kent. It's a girls' school that takes boarders from the age of seven ...

Charlotte's story

Charlotte, 11, has been boarding since September 2001. She goes home every weekend ...

'Before I came here, I lived in Poland for two years and, before that, in Germany. Right now, my family live 20 minutes away, but they'll have to go abroad again soon cos of my stepdad's job. Which is why I'm here - it's good training for when I can't go home every weekend. I don't think I'd want to be a full-time boarder just yet - I still get a bit homesick.

'Going to boarding school is something I've worried about cos of all the travelling my family does. When I was six, I made Mum promise not to send me to one, so at first I was shocked at the thought of coming here. I would rather be with my family. But this is the best thing - it gives me stability. Plus, it's nice to make friends who are gonna be around for a while.

'The people here are really kind, which made it easy to settle in. Although after a few weeks I did miss home. I rang my mum a lot and tried to think about the good points of being here. At least I'm on my family's doorstep - it must be a lot harder for the girls whose families live abroad. Compared to them, I'd call myself a coward. I never see them getting upset.

'I like sharing a room cos I'm never lonely, but it can be stressful. I went to a mixed school before and I miss having lads around. You don't always feel like talking about girlie stuff! It's a great place to socialise though, and I'm definitely more independent now - it's like one big sleepover. But if my family lived in Britain permanently, I'd prefer to be a day girl instead.'

Text 2

Memory

Memory, recall and recollection are words in everyday use. Memory relates to the ability of living organisms to think about (relive) past experiences. Researchers have claimed that memory has four components

- Learning – how we gain new information and skills;
- Retention – how we store the new knowledge;
- Recall – how we remember the knowledge, when it is needed; and
- Recognition – how we determine which information is needed and when.

Many of the early ideas about memory were developed from studies of short- and long-term memory, in which researchers examined how long it took their subjects to learn and forget novel pieces of information. Much of the early writing seemed to describe memory as a place in the brain where information was held and, of course, sometimes lost.

Contemporary views of memory, mainly established through the study and results of electrical stimulation of the brain through an open skull, and through work with amnesics, have convinced researchers that memories are not held in any one place in the brain. Rather, memory involves complex electrochemical changes in the brain creating electrical networks which reflect what we see in our mind's eye. This suggests the dynamic and strategic nature of memory and, hence, learning.

From *Using Cognitive Methods in the Classroom* by A. Ashman and R. Conway

Text 3

CAULIFLOWER CHEESE AND MUSTARD SOUP

This is a soup for cold winter evenings. Creamy, hot and substantial, it is not an elegant soup, but one for eating from deep bowls. Use any cheese, so long as it has bags of flavour – the louder the better.

Serves 4

50g butter
a medium onion, peeled and chopped
2 cloves of garlic, peeled and crushed
2 small or 1 large cauliflower, broken into florets
2 bay leaves
a large potato, peeled and cubed
4 tablespoons crème fraîche
a heaped tablespoon of grain mustard

To finish:
2 thick slices of bread, cut into 1cm cubes
50g butter
200g punchy farmhouse Cheddar, grated

Melt the butter in a deep pan. Add the onion and garlic and fry until soft, but do not let them colour. Meanwhile, boil the cauliflower florets for six to eight minutes, until almost tender. Add the bay leaves to the onion, then the cauliflower and its cooking water and the potato. Bring to the boil and add salt. Simmer for 15 minutes.

Remove from the heat, fish out the bay leaves and purée the soup in a blender, mouli or food processor. Pour back into the plan. Stir in the crème fraîche, mustard and a grinding of black pepper. Bring back to the boil. Fry the bread cubes in the butter until golden.

Ladle the soup into warm bowls, stir in the cheese, taste – adding more salt, pepper or mustard as you wish – and scatter over the croûtons.

ACTIVITY 10

Now look at the three texts below and on pages 21–22.

What do you notice about the way the writers attempt to draw attention to the main points in their material? Use a table like the one below to record your ideas. Tick the appropriate presentational device(s) used in each text, and then, in pairs, discuss the reasons each device is used and how effective it is.

Presentational device	Text 1	Text 2	Text 3
Illustrations			
Headlines			
Sub-headings			
Bold			
Different colours			
Logos			

Text 1

ORLANDO

Orlando, the fun capital of the USA! A magical mix of sun, shopping and theme parks – sure to bring out the child in you!

CITYFILE

SIGHTSEEING

Disney® Magic Kingdom, Wet 'n' Wild, Seaworld and Universal – need we say more – there is plenty to do and see. Entrance prices vary from approx £20pp for Wet 'n' Wild and approx £32pp for Disney (this is exclusive of tax) for one day tickets. These entrance tickets are not included in the price of your holiday but can be easily obtained whilst on holiday.

SHOPPING

Orlando is fantastic for shopping including Disney Village, Balz Factory Outlet Mall (one of the largest in the country) and Florida Mall.

TRANSFERS

Transfers are not included in the price of your holiday. You can take a taxi from the airport costing approx £25 per taxi.

Wyndham Orlando   TTTT

Located on lively International Drive, the Wyndham Orlando Resort is only minutes from Universal Studios, Wet and Wild water park and Sea World. There is also 'Chelsea's' for breakfast, lunch and dinner along with 'Marmalade Tree' for food and drink while you are lounging poolside.

LOCATION • Centrally located for the nightlife and attractions on International Drive

FACILITIES • 3 outdoor pools, whirlpool and tennis courts. All rooms have private facilities, telephone, TV and air-cond. There is a daily complimentary shuttle to Universal Studios, Sea World and Wet and Wild.

Room: 1,064

Hotel Code: R4ORL   Map Ref: 2

Clarion Universal   TTT

Ⓒ A well located and full service hotel. For convenience 'Sharky and Jack's Bar and Grill' is open for breakfast/dinner. The cabana poolside bar is a great place to relax and have a drink.

LOCATION • Conveniently located just around the corner from the entertainment, shopping and nightlife of International Drive • Steps away from Wet and Wild water park · 8 miles from Disney World.

FACILITIES • Heated swimming pool, 2 whirlpools, tennis court • All rooms have air-con., coffee-maker, hairdryer, safe, ironing board • There is a complimentary daily bus shuttle to Universal Studios and Sea World.

Rooms: 303

Hotel Code: OR3CLA   Map Ref: 1

Wyndham Palace Resort   TTTTT

This Wyndham resort is located in the Walt Disney World® Resort and a short walk to Downtown Disney. Arthur's 27 is the Palace's award winning restaurant with panoramic Floridian views for evening dining.

LOCATION • In the heart of Walt Disney World® Resort and a short walk to Downtown Disney attractions.

FACILITIES • Spa, 3 heated pools, fitness centre, tennis courts, bars and restaurants, including 'Arthur's 27'. A special feature is the complimentary shuttle to Disney World's attractions and the four Disney World parks and two water parks.

Rooms: 1,014

Hotel Code: OR5PAL   Map Ref: 3

Prices from £409

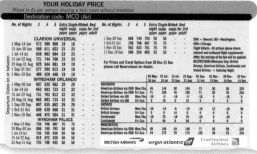

Text 2

Tell your friends you're going travelling in India.

Just don't tell them it's from one luxury hotel to another.

Let your friends think you're being terribly adventurous. Let them think you want to be stimulated, challenged and amazed by the spiritualism of the land that gave birth to yoga. That you want a holiday that doesn't simply give you a suntan, but one which opens the mind and enriches the soul.

Let them think all these things, because they are all true of India.

But, then again, maybe you don't need to add that you'll be staying in the cosseted confines of some of the world's finest hotels.

That you'll reflect on the wondrous sights you've seen as you lie by the pool in the gardens of a maharajah's palace. Or an ex-colonial stately home. Or a lodge in the verdant foothills. Or a stunning beach-side resort.

The fact is, India is a land of contradictions. And indulging your desire for adventure while also living in unashamed luxury is just another of them.

For more details, simply ring 0870 010 2183 or visit our website.

भारत
India
www.indiatouristoffice.org

21

Text 3

ON THE ROAD

'ULLO JOHN, WANT A NEW MOTOR? IF YOU DO, BE WARNED: WHEN BUYING A CAR, THE ROAD FROM DEALER'S FORECOURT TO THE SAFETY OF YOUR GARAGE IS NOT ALWAYS A SMOOTH ONE

IT'S ALL BRAND NEW

You're at the dealers, expecting to take delivery of your gorgeous, shiny new car. You ordered a rather flash 4WD in arctic silver with air-conditioning, CD player and one of those handy little holders that keep your coffee upright. Except when it turns up, the colour is less arctic silver, more muddy snow. 'Nothing to do with me, mate,' says your friendly neighbourhood dealer, when you point this out. 'You're going to have to go back to the manufacturer on this one.'

 You certainly do not have to go back to the manufacturer. Your contract was with the retailer – the dealer – and so it's their responsibility to make sure that the car is of satisfactory quality, bearing in mind the way it was described and how much it cost. This covers, among other things, the appearance and finish of the car. So if you were told you were buying a silver car, a silver car is what he should get you. The only time you should go back to the manufacturer, by the way – other than if a problem is covered by a manufacturer's guarantee – is if the car was unsafe, and caused damage to you or your property.

Rather disappointed, you drive the car home. It's the first really hot day of the year, so you quite quickly discover that the air conditioning only works if you're doing over 50mph. To try and lift your mood, you pop a CD into the player. And then it jams on track one. What does your dealer say? 'You drove it away, didn't you? Sorry, that's acceptance.'

 Unfortunately, they've got a point. It's vital that you inspect a new car on delivery, as driving the car away can be deemed as 'acceptance' – which means that your chances of getting a replacement or compensation may be reduced.

However, an express term of the contract was that the colour of the car would be silver; and an implied term was that the CD would work. The dealer has broken the contract, so although you've taken the car home, the contract is not binding and you're free to return the car.

In this instance, you can either cancel the financial agreement or withhold payment until the dealer agrees to provide you with the car you originally contracted to buy.

THE CAR WAS MEANT TO BE SILVER – THE DEALER HAS BROKEN THE CONTRACT

Read critically

Sometimes, newspapers and the media in general blur the distinction between fact and opinion in order to provoke a particular response from their targeted audience.

 REMEMBER

Ask yourself the three questions:

✦ Who is the intended audience?   ✦ What is the purpose?

✦ What techniques does the writer use?

The text below provides a light-hearted example of personal opinion being presented as factual information.

HOW TO ...
USE A TAXI
GUY BROWNING

There are two types of taxis: cabs that smell of essence of vanilla are owned by the driver; cabs that smell of the compost of humanity are rented by the driver. Taxi drivers also fall into two types: those who talk in a friendly way at the beginning of the journey because they like talking, and those who talk in a friendly way at the end of the journey because they like tipping.

When you're talking to a cabbie, you have to decide whether to look at the back of the driver's neck or at his eyes in the rear-view mirror. If you do a bit of both, you come away with the spooky impression that the driver has eyes in the back of his head.

Backs of cabs are a fantastic place to pounce on the person you fancy. It's relatively private, but not so private that you can't immediately stop, get out and be public again. (Interestingly, a good snog lasts about £1.60 on the meter of a black cab.)

Hailing a cab is often awkward for the British, who have been trained from birth not to flap their arms around like excitable continentals. Ideally, cabbies would notice when you did a cool little flicking movement with your hand. In reality, the cabbie will be mesmerised by the man on the other side of the street doing the impression of a heron taking off.

The last quarter of any taxi journey is spent praying the meter will stop on an amount that allows you to give one note and say a breezy 'keep the change'. Cabbies are wise to this, and will drive a route guaranteed to finish when the fare is five pence over the note, forcing you to give a cripplingly large tip.

Being driven around in the back of a cab is the nearest most of us will get to the sensation of being royal. The only difference is that taxis don't have police outriders, so you'll probably be stuck in traffic waving at the same person for five minutes. You also won't have people waving back at you, except for the idiots who haven't noticed the yellow light is off.

From *The Guardian Weekend*

ACTIVITY 11

1 Look through copies of newspapers and magazines to find your own examples of where the blurring between fact and fiction is done for a more serious purpose.

2 In groups, discuss how the writers in your examples achieve their effects and what might be their purpose for doing so. If you are studying a text such as *Animal Farm* for English Literature you could cross-refer to that.

Following an argument

Often when we refer to an argument we mean a heated exchange of views between two or more people.

However, in writing, an **argument** means something rather different – it is a series of statements or **reasons** that lead logically to a **conclusion** or **point of view** on a particular subject. In an argument, you try to convince your readers that your point of view makes sense, and you usually do this by giving a number of reasons for any opinions you offer.

For example, you could be asked to write an argument for or against:

- school uniform
- the use of mobile phones
- homework
- the death penalty
- medical experiments on animals
- legalising cannabis
- any other controversial issue.

You will come across written arguments every day – in newspapers, magazines, textbooks and elsewhere. The ability to select relevant information is particularly useful when you are trying to evaluate a writer's argument. It helps you to separate fact from opinion and to identify more easily the writer's point of view.

Point of view

A writer's point of view is often implied rather than directly stated. This can be achieved in various ways, for example by:

- choice of vocabulary
- use of quotations.

ACTIVITY 12

Working in groups, look at these two headlines:

President murdered by terrorists

President assassinated by Freedom Fighters

How does the choice of vocabulary convey different meanings?

Quoting the views of someone else allows writers to criticise a viewpoint or to use it to present their own opinions while seeming to remain objective.

ACTIVITY 13

Read carefully the newspaper article below and on page 26.

1 Put into your own words the viewpoints of the people the writer refers to.

2 Say what you think the writer's point of view might be. (Look closely at her choice of words and the way that quotations have been selected.)

3 Make a list of the facts and opinions contained in the article. Are there any places where you are not sure whether you have a fact or opinion? Why?

Why your make-up bag may be making you ill

ALARMING new research has shown the extent to which toxic chemicals lurk in your cosmetics. These toxins could cause cancer, induce comas or, in extreme cases, cause death. GOOD HEALTH investigates.

By
ALICE
FOWLER

EVERY day, women are unknowingly exposing themselves to a cocktail of toxic chemicals – just by following a beauty regime, it has been claimed.

According to controversial new research, make-up bags and bathroom shelves are loaded with seemingly innocent products which, over time, can cause cancer, disrupt hormones or break down into formaldehyde.

The claims are laid bare in a new book, Drop Dead Gorgeous: Protecting Yourself From The Hidden Dangers Of Cosmetics, published in Britain next month. Its authors, Kim Erickson and Samuel Epstein, say modern cosmetics are packed with chemicals more at home in a test tube than on our faces.

'These synthetic ingredients are inexpensive, stable and have a long shelf-life,' says Erickson, an American environmental journalist. 'Manufacturers love them but, though the majority appear safe in the short run, the results from long-term use could be deadly.'

Up to 60 per cent of any substance applied to the skin is absorbed by the body. Eye make-up, for example, can be absorbed by the highly sensitive mucous membranes, while hair sprays, perfumes and dusting powders can be inhaled.

We may all be suffering a toxic chemical overload, producing symptoms such as headaches, nausea and fatigue.

But such claims are dismissed by the British beauty industry.

'It's a criminal offence to place a cosmetic product on the market if it's liable to cause damage to human health,' says Marion Kelly, director of the Cosmetic, Toiletry and Perfumery Association (CTPA), the UK industry's trade body.

'European manufacturers have an obligation to carry out a safety assessment, taking into account the product, ingredients used and any interactions between them.

'If there was a concern about short-term or long-term reaction, the safety assessor would not sign it off. Consumers have nothing to worry about.'

Yet many disagree. Four years ago, Margaret Marrone – a homeopath and qualified pharmacist – began to investigate ingredients in skincare products.

Continues on page 26.

25

She is concerned about the wetting agents diethanolamine (DEA) and triethanolamine (TEA), found in shampoos, body and face washes, and which have been linked to cancer.

'They're not carcinogenic in themselves,' she emphasises. 'But there's a chemical reaction that can take place as the product sits on the shelf, which release nitrosamines and those *are* carcinogenic.'

But are such ingredients really harmful? Or are these claims simply scaremongering, an attempt to play on consumers' fears?

The CTPA's Marion Kelly says: 'DEA and TEA have a potential to form nitrosamines which are carcinogenic, but strict manufacturing controls are in place to ensure that nitrosamines formation does not occur.'

She argues that we encounter more carcinogens eating burnt toast or crossing a road than we do in a lifetime's use of beauty products.

Even so, allergies and skin sensitivity cases are on the rise. The Breakspear Hospital has seen 8,000 women, almost all of whom were found to have a sensitivity to cosmetics, since it opened in 1982.

The Consumers' Association has criticised the way that, while cosmetic manufacturers are obliged by law to list ingredients, fragrance chemicals are excluded.

Any of 2,600 such chemicals can be listed under the catch-all term '*parfum*', despite 24 of these having been identified by the European Union Scientific Committee For Cosmetics and Non-Food Products as a common cause of allergies.

Meanwhile, many companies selling organic or natural products are reporting huge increases in sales.

Perhaps, just as with food, that increased awareness by the public can only be for the better.

Additional research by Amy Anderson

GIVE YOUR COSMETIC CASE A MAKEOVER

Blushers, eye-liners and mascara

BLUSHERS and eye-liners often contain an artificial colouring – coal tar, which can be absorbed and stored in our organs and fatty tissues. For some sensitive people, coal tar colours can cause such symptoms as nausea, headaches, skin problems, fatigue and mood swings. Coal tar dyes have produced cancer in laboratory animals.

Eye shadows

MANY eye shadows contain artificial colours, which have been shown to cause cancer if applied directly to the skin.

Liquid foundations

MANY liquid foundations contain nitrosamines, which are highly carcinogenic. Some foundations contain lanolin, a softening agent that can be contaminated with carcinogenic pesticides.

Cream foundations and cream eye shadows

CREAM foundations often contain the specific preservative propylparaben, which some reports say is cancer-causing.

Lipsticks

MOST lipsticks contain petrolatum, a gelling agent derived from petroleum, which can cause dryness. Lipsticks also contain high levels of artificial colourings, some of which are harmful if ingested because they are carcinogenic. One woman can ingest up to 60 kilos of lipstick in a lifetime if she wears it daily.

Isopropyl alcohol is used in some lipsticks. It is also lipophilic – it is attracted to the lipid layer surrounding the cells and nerves. The lipid fluids cannot line up properly in the presence of these chemicals and can in turn create neurological effects and damage to the cells.

Cosmetics and beauty-care products that do not contain any of the above chemicals are on the rise as manufacturers take responsibility for what is in their products. Readily available 'chemical-free' cosmetics include Aveda, Origins, The Body Shop and Neal's Yard products.

Selecting and collating material

Selecting

In the exam you will need to show that you have understood what you have read by **selecting** information related to a particular point. To do this you will have to focus on what is relevant and eliminate from your writing anything that either does not relate directly to your point or repeats an argument unnecessarily.

KEY POINTS

Make use of all the help the material gives you. For example:

- There may be sub-headings in the article that help you to summarise the important points.

- There may be quotations emphasising key points interspersed with the text.

- Key points may be written in bold or italic type.

Focusing like this will help you to structure your answer. Read the whole article through quickly to gain an overall understanding of its content. Once you have done this, read over it again but this time try to filter out what is not relevant to the information you have been asked to select. Then underline or highlight those words and phrases which are relevant. Next, you can start to make notes.

ACTIVITY 14

Read the article on page 28 and then list key points under the following headings.

The causes of stress to students	What parents and students can do to relieve the stress

Result!

Few things will cause as much conflict between you and your kids as school. So how can you help your kids get the most from those all-important school years without pushing them too hard?

Ease the pressure

There's a lot of pressure on teenagers to succeed academically, so the last thing parents should do is add to those pressures by expecting too much. 'Parental pressure – when parents ask the child to achieve a standard that they're really unable to do – could be counterproductive,' says teacher Nancy Morse, who has taught in France, the US and the UK, and recently founded online educational resource www.parentlink.co.uk. 'Parental support should be positive at all times.'

The first thing parents can do to help is to create an environment and atmosphere at home that is conducive to learning. One basic, practical necessity, says Morse, is to 'ensure your child has a quiet, comfortable place to work, away from distractions.'

They should be encouraged to use their study space regularly, and establish a routine that's rigid, if not entirely unbreakable. 'Try not to lay down the law,' says Dr Diana Wilson, an educational researcher and former teacher. 'The key is to negotiate the time spent on homework. Once the time has been agreed between you, it should be kept. But do allow for some flexibility, when there's a good reason.'

Getting the balance right

There's a big difference between creating a good learning environment for your children and pushing them beyond their capabilities or capacity to learn. Teachers know that parental support and encouragement is the foundation for academic achievement. They also know unreasonable pressure can be destructive. 'Parents can belittle their child's achievements in a misguided attempt to make them do even better,' says Dr Wilson.

Children who feel under constant pressure to satisfy the ambitions of parents can get discouraged, show signs of stress and become depressed and withdrawn from family life. Some will deliberately under-achieve as a way of getting back at pushy parents or just to lower expectations. Others will rebel openly – drinking, taking drugs or running away from home. None of these symptoms is necessarily the result of parental pressure, but expecting too much from an overstretched teen can lead to problems.

It's worth remembering one basic rule. 'There are many ways of helping a child to do well,' says teacher and counsellor Lynda Finn, 'but nothing is more effective than boosting that child's self-esteem and confidence.'

Organising time

Angela Vincent, who has taught in secondary schools in England and Australia for 35 years, says: 'The most important factor is not to let work build up and get out of control. When children let this happen, it puts them off even trying, as the volume of the workload becomes daunting. When children can't face up to their tasks, bad habits arise, such as panicking and doing everything at the last minute.'

Establishing good habits is particularly important to get kids into the habit of working at a consistent pace, even if they have to force themselves at first. Once these good habits have been formed, they'll be programmed to carry on.

Let them have some fun

It's not just parents who push children too hard – schools can too. Lynda Finn says that kids have a right to be kids – meeting friends, watching TV or simply chilling out. The best way for parents to ensure their children are working hard, but not too hard, is to communicate, with both the child and the school.

Finn recommends that, in some cases, a much stronger relationship needs to exist between parents and school. Look out for the symptoms. If you think your child is doing too much or too little, or you have concerns about their academic progress generally, don't wait until the parents' evening – speak to the school straight away.

Communicating with the school is essential, and so is communicating with the child. If teachers report behavioural problems, parents shouldn't rush to condemn a child for what could be a symptom of a deeper emotional issue. 'The child must be sure the parent is on their side,' Lynda Finn says. 'That's not to say the parent should insist that the child is always right, but to make it clear that come what may, the child is loved and valued, even if they've done something wrong.

'If, for example, a child knows the parent is going to punish them the moment the school says: "He hasn't handed in homework for a month," then he won't open up about what drove him to it in the first place.'

It's good to talk

James Windell, a psychotherapist and parenting expert, makes the surprising but encouraging observation that, although teenagers want their independence, 'surveys show adolescents also want to communicate more with their parents.' He reckons 'The key is always for parents to avoid giving answers or advice or make assumptions, but just to listen to what their children have to say.'

From *Total Guide to Teenagers* by Hugh Wilson

Collating

As well as selecting information, you may also be asked to **collate** it. This means that you will need to read more than one piece of writing on a similar subject, select all relevant information and then combine all the points together for a specific purpose.

ACTIVITY 15

Read the material below and on pages 30–31. Using the notes you made in Activity 14, produce a guide for parents, informing them of the problems their children may come across during Years 10 and 11 and giving advice on ways to cope with them.

REMEMBER

+ Select information.
+ Organise your notes under different headings.
+ Make sure you distinguish between facts and opinions.
+ Use your own words whenever possible.
+ Write in an appropriate register.

'Real Lives'

'When Sam first started secondary school he became exhausted as he struggled to keep up with the huge homework load and produce great work in every subject,' says his dad Daniel Micklethwaite. 'After a while we realised he needed to ease off and as long as he got it done, it couldn't all be brilliant.' Unless your children work around the clock, they won't be able to produce first-rate work in every subject. There just isn't time. Suggest they concentrate on excelling in Geography one week, History the next and so on. Homework should be part of the learning process, not just another pressure to strive for perfection.

'I once got so involved with daughter Sara's science project that I became fanatical about it,' says Rosemarie Henshall. 'I put her off doing it in the end. I found her loads of information from different sources but she just got it all out of one book. I felt really upset and resentful of all the time I'd spent.' It's important you don't get too obsessive about your child's work, and don't hover over them while they're doing it. Be aware of what they're doing and always be ready to listen. If they show a glimmer of interest in any subject then follow it up. Remember: you're just there to help, not to take over.

Cause for concern?

Isobel Turnbull was worried that her son Matthew, 13, was being bullied by his best friend. A visit to the school helped to ease the situation enormously.

'Don't go into the school on the attack,' she says. 'You need to say, "My child is having a problem. How can we work this out?" Start with the teacher, never the head. It's important not to undermine the teacher's authority. If you really feel that you're not making any progress, ask for the parent governor to sit in on the discussion with the head. This is only necessary in extreme cases, but every school has two parent governors and acting as a neutral witness to such discussions is part of their job.

'In my case the teacher was unaware of the problem, so it was a worthwhile visit. She kept a close eye on what was going on and was sensitive to Matthew's dilemma.

'However, I also approached the mother of the other boy about this issue, as well as the school, and this caused all kinds of problems. Don't, under any circumstances, do this. Stick to the proper channels.'

From *Total Guide to Teenagers* by Hugh Wilson

Dealing with your child's teachers

If there's a problem, you'll need to talk to your child's teachers. Here teacher Angela Vincent gives some tips on how to get the most out of your meeting

Phone the school and ask to speak to the form teacher, the head of year or the teacher in charge of pastoral care. Make an appointment to see one of these three. The school will suggest which is most suitable. There's no point in trying to see the head teacher at this stage, unless something really awful has occurred. Start with a teacher who knows your child fairly well.

Don't go in with guns blazing, no matter how indignant you are. This will only antagonise the teachers. You need to be calm and tactful.

'Personality clash' is the key phrase in child/teacher disputes. Don't go in and say: 'My son hates his English teacher.' Instead try: 'I think there's a slight personality clash between my son and his teacher.' The form teacher will probably consult the specific teacher at this stage for their account of the situation. There are two sides to every story.

It's natural to side with your child, but try not to show that you're totally supportive of him or her. Bear the teacher in mind. Teachers are people too and it's possible that your son or daughter has been exaggerating, if only slightly. You need to find out the truth.

If bullying is the issue, you'll certainly find a sympathetic ear. Schools are now very hot on this subject and usually have a special policy. You need to be as specific and honest as possible.

If the problem at the root of it all is a general difficulty with work, rather than a particular subject, raise the possibility of your child moving groups or changing to a lower set in some subjects. There's no shame in doing this and it could help their long-term chances of academic success.

If you don't get the response you want, you'll need to contact the school governors or the local education authority. However, it's unlikely you'll need to take matters this far. Schools are generally very responsive to parents' concerns and will much prefer to solve the problem at grass roots level.

From *Total Guide to Teenagers* by Hugh Wilson

5 Ways to get great results

Advice from teacher Angela Vincent

1 Buy a wall planner

Put it up in a place where you can all see it and encourage your children to make a homework plan. Rather than imposing a timetable on them, which they'll resent, let the children lead the way. They're learning time-management here – a skill which will serve them well in later life. They can plan a week or two weeks ahead, working out how much time each day they're going to spend on their homework, and then stick to it. But it's vital that the plan includes time for leisure activity. Children need something to look forward to while they're working.

2 Feed the brain

Break up the work schedule with healthy snacks. Make sure they have something to eat when they get home from school, before they start their homework. It'll give them the energy they need to continue working. This doesn't have to mean junk food, although chocolate is a good short-term energy source. Keep healthy snacks like cherry tomatoes or chopped up raw vegetables in the fridge as well as loads of fruit. Buy mini-samosas or onion bhajis from the supermarket as an alternative to crisps. Make sure there's plenty of bottled water in the fridge too.

3 Do something physical

Youngsters need to intersperse work with physical activity. This is especially important for boys, who have loads of physical energy and won't be able to concentrate until they've used some of it up. This can range from kicking a ball around the garden to doing some simple stretching exercises indoors. The main objective is to move around and loosen up as an antidote to all that time spent sitting still.

4 Keep it brief

Don't make them work for too long. Realistically they'll only concentrate properly for about 25 minutes before the brain starts to flag. So if your children have allocated two hours for homework, suggest they break up the time into segments punctuated by five minutes exercise or snack breaks.

5 Build in room for flexibility

Allow for the fact that a social engagement might crop up during the week. If a child misses out on homework time one night, they need to make space to catch up on another one. Encourage them to work this out for themselves and don't tell them they can't go. They need to have fun and pleasure too, otherwise they'll become jaded. Remember: you're not running an army camp. Life may throw your children a curve ball and they may not be able to stick to their timetable. But at least if they devise one – according to their own specifications – you're off to a good start.

From *Total Guide to Teenagers* by Hugh Wilson

The writer's techniques

A writer may use various techniques to produce the effect s/he intends.
We are going to look at **vocabulary**, **register** and **structure**.

Vocabulary

Vocabulary means the words the writer uses. The type of vocabulary used
by a writer influences the tone of his/her piece. For example, if the writing
contains a large number of long words it is likely to have a formal tone.

ACTIVITY 16

1   Look at the list of words in the table below that could be used to describe a
    writer's vocabulary. Copy the table and write your own definition of each word
    (use a dictionary if necessary). Look for examples of each type of vocabulary in
    all the texts you've just been reading and then comment on the effects the
    writers achieve.

Cauliflower cheese and
mustard soup

Because you care about
a child who is suffering

5 Ways to get great results!

What about the people who live there 24/7?

Vocabulary	Definition	Example	Effect
Formal			
Informal			
Colloquial			
Didactic			
Technical			
Emotive			
Abstract			
Concrete			
Precise			
Vague			

2   Now think of some information texts of your own and consider how suited the
    author's vocabulary is to meet his/her purpose. For example, an instruction
    manual is likely to be written using formal vocabulary, whereas an
    advertisement is more likely to use emotive or colloquial words.

3   Try rewriting one of your example texts using a totally different type of
    vocabulary and then write an explanation of the effect you have achieved.

Register

Register is the term used to describe the way writers make their writing interesting and accessible to their intended audience.

A writer's tone of voice (serious, light-hearted, formal, etc.) is one way in which register is communicated. The following features are also important to the creation of an appropriate register:

- vocabulary
- the length of sentences and paragraphs
- the similes and metaphors the writer chooses (see Unit 2, page 75)
- the **pronoun** by which the reader is addressed
- the form of the verbs in the passage, for example, think how using the **imperative** form of the verb, in 'First wash your hands' creates a more formal register than the instruction, 'You might first like to wash your hands'.

ACTIVITY 17

Below is a list of words that could be used to describe register.

1 Write a definition of each word (use a dictionary if necessary).

2 Now write a paragraph on the subject 'A Guide to the School Canteen' in as many different registers as you can.

Register	Definition
Formal	
Informal	
Biased	
Colloquial	
Humorous/witty	
Serious	
Patronising	
Friendly	
Thought-provoking	

Structure

In evaluating the effectiveness of a text, you need to think about the way a writer structures his/her material. In particular, look at the ways writers construct sentences and paragraphs.

 **ACTIVITY 18**

Working in groups, look back at what you wrote for Activity 17 and discuss how you achieved the different effects. Consider, in particular, the use of the following techniques:

- short direct sentences
- long involved sentences
- short (one- or two-sentence) paragraphs
- long paragraphs
- sub-headings.

 **ACTIVITY 19**

Read carefully the two articles about Walt Disney Studios Paris on pages 35–36 and then compare the information they provide and the ways in which it is presented. How successful have they been in making you want to visit the theme park? Give reasons based on your analysis of the articles.

You could organise your answer using the following plan.

Step 1	Identify the **audience** for and **purpose** of each article.
Step 2	Explain how the layout of the articles and the use of **presentational devices** help to attract the intended audience.
Step 3	What are the main **facts** and **opinions** contained in each article? (Can you find any facts that are mentioned in both?)
Step 4	Consider the features of the theme park described by each writer and the **writer's attitude** towards them.
Step 5	Think about each writer's **tone** and **register**. How is this conveyed by the use of language? Is the register formal or informal?
Step 6	Look closely at each writer's **choice of words**. How effective are they for their purpose?
Step 7	Refer your points back to the question and explain why you would (or would not) like to visit the park.

Article 1

New Walt Disney Studios® Park

Disney Studio 1

Laugh, clap and marvel at a tribute to the best of Tinsel Town. You're on set in Disney Studio 1 for the shooting of a motion picture production. Props, sets and famous facades surround you. It's your moment to shine!

As if Disneyland® Resort Paris isn't amazing enough, on March 16th 2002, there is even more to celebrate. The brand new Walt Disney Studios® Park opens right next to Disneyland® Park – you'll be spoilt for choice! But you don't have to choose – enjoy them both in a feast of entertainment.

A visit to the Walt Disney Studios® Park will take you into the exciting world of film and television, through four zones packed with action and spectacular sights and experiences. You'll also get to meet the new Disney stars, including those from the new film *Monsters Inc.* which is due to be released in the Spring.

Wanna be in the movies? Start at **Front Lot**, where you'll enjoy a thrilling tribute to the best of Tinsel Town. Then stroll up **Hollywood Boulevard** to the soundstage, filled with lights and movie sets. You never know who you might meet – and you may get to be a star.

In the **Animation Courtyard** you can watch your favourite Disney moments come to life in Animagique – amazing! – then see how the greatest animations of all time are created at the Art of Disney Animation. And once you've watched the experts at work, you can have a go yourself. Finish your visit with a ride aboard the Genie's magical carpet and let your imagination fly.

In the **Production Courtyard** you can get a behind-the-scenes take on what could be tomorrow's blockbuster movie. Celebrate the best of 100 years of movies in CinéMagique, then it's all aboard for the Studio Tram Tour featuring Catastrophe Canyon to see where movie magic is made. Discover how special effects are created and see costumes, props and vehicles from some of your favourite Disney cinema classics. Then hold on to your hats as the Tour takes a detour through Catastrophe Canyon for real-life movie experience. And that's not all! Take the Television Production Tour into the wonderful world of TV and watch a live studio production at the Walt Disney TV Studios.

Complete your visit with a trip to **Backlot**. There the spectacular space station from the blockbuster *Armageddon* will take you for a special-effects extravaganza. Then enjoy the Stunt Show Spectacular as speeding cars and motorcycles involve you in a high-speed chase. Finally, buckle up and ride the music as the Rock 'n' Roller Coaster starring Aerosmith takes you all the way – and then some!

© Disney

Disneyland® Park

The five enchanting lands in Disneyland® Park are just a short walk from Walt Disney Studios® Park. Your experience starts in **Main Street, U.S.A.** where you can meet Mickey, Minnie and Co and enjoy the various Parades. **Frontierland** is the largest of the lands with a Wild West theme and spectacular Arizona landscape. Take a wild ride on Big Thunder Mountain and scare yourself in Phantom Manor.

Adventureland combines a taste of the Caribbean, the desert and the jungle with the thrilling rollercoaster ride Indiana Jones (TM) and the Temple of Peril: Backwards! and the Pirates of the Caribbean boat ride.

The Sleeping Beauty Castle in **Fantasyland** is the main landmark of Disneyland® Park. Most of the attractions are designed for younger guests, such as Dumbo the Flying Elephant and Peter Pan's Flight.

Intergalactic voyages, special effects and the history of inventions await visitors to **Discoveryland**. Space Mountain and Honey, I Shrunk The Audience are a must. And if that's not enough, Disney® Village has shops, restaurants and nightspots to keep the fun going well into the night.

With so much to see and do it makes sense to stay a while. There are excellent Disneyland® Resort Paris themed hotels and log cabins, and other hotels near the magic. It all adds up to the perfect trip – so make this the year the magic happens to you.

Article 2

WALT DISNEY STUDIOS, PARIS

Andrew Eames and family visit the new Walt Disney Studios

ARMAGEDDON didn't happen for us. We got so close we could almost smell the fear, but right at the last moment, when the world was about to be blasted into smithereens, there was a tug at my sleeve. The combination of extreme excitement and queuing in a cold wind had taken its toll on eight-year-old Thomas's bladder, and he was desperate. So Armageddon became Armagettin'-off, and I can now tell my friends, in all seriousness, that I was saved from witnessing the end of the world by my son's need for a wee.

We were in Walt Disney Studios, the latest creation of the world's most skilful imagineers, and new sister for the Disneyland park just outside Paris. We adults were trying to maintain a sense of cool and critical detachment, but our children were so hyper it was as if they'd been magicked into cartoons themselves. At one point, Thomas became so impossibly animated that we sent him running up and down the hotel corridor to work off some steam.

Personally, I am not a willing disciple of theme parks, and emerging into the neon and concrete of the unappealing Disney Village restaurant, bar and shopping area, where even the air smelled deep-fried, reminded me of a teacher who used to warn us against the hollowness of 'synthetic fun'. The best things in life, he maintained, are free but Disney is synthetic fun from wall to wall and ear to ear – and there is something in my education, my generation, and my wallet, that resists it.

This particular set of pseudo-Studios cost £400 million to create, which is cheap for a world attraction but in comparison with Disneyland Paris next door, it isn't particularly large. Disney-watchers also point out that it contains little that is different from its cousin across the pond. To my mind, its size does make the entrance fee disproportionately expensive, even allowing for the fact that you can make an evening visit to Disneyland in the summer when the Studios close at 8pm and the main park stays open to 11pm.

I have to say that the success of the Paris Studios is mixed. We started off on a tram tour in the company of video commentary from Jeremy Irons. It sounded as if he was trying to be enthusiastic about the planes from *Pearl Harbor* and robots from *Dinosaur*, but the problem was, they just looked like rusty bits of scrap. It seems that, these days, films use a lot of computer-generated images and fewer real 'things'. Whatever, the lumps of metal along the roadside had no charisma for us.

Then came Animagique, a Disney cartoon stage show, which was, in effect, a luminous ballet of foam-rubber Disney characters with extra pink elephants thrown in for good measure. Rhena, my six-year-old daughter, liked it but I prefer watching the cartoons – surely the whole point of cartoons is the fact that they're not real and you can watch steamrollered cats picking themselves up off the floor. Rhena was a bit less sure about Cinemagique, in which a member of the audience was cleverly drawn into scenes from famous movies. Her main concern was: how would they get out again?

To my mind, movie-based theme parks work best when they imitate action-adventure films, and this one reaches maximum thrust in the stunt show, Moteurs Action, performed to a football stadium-sized arena of 3,000 people, some of whom had started queuing an hour before . . . It is already the Studios' biggest draw, and it is worth knowing when it's on, because it soaks up so many visitors that queues elsewhere diminish.

Even at its busiest time, however, you are unlikely to get a whole day or even a whole visit out of Walt Disney Studios, a fact which Disney itself acknowledges in its slogan 'Twice Upon a Time', the implication being that you will do both parks at one bite, and I'm sure they're right – who is going to come here and just do one? The children will feel deprived and the parents mean, so shelling out for both is inevitable, if painful.

The other implication of the 'Twice Upon a Time' slogan is that the Disney experience is already so firmly ensconced in the consciousness of today's child that it has become part of traditional story-telling. I must admit that I rather resented that hijacking of the phrase, but there is definitely something of the fairytale about the main park, which we'd never visited before.

Disneyland Park itself is manicured, detailed, aesthetically pleasing and carefully crafted; I'd happily sign up these builders to do my loft conversion, minus the furry ears. There's nothing tawdry about it, the scenery doesn't quiver when bumped, the litter-pickers wear bow-ties, the electrical parade is beautiful, and there's always the feeling, when you leave an attraction, that you didn't quite take in all the intricacies of what you were experiencing, so you really need to do it again. The big set pieces, from Space Mountain to It's a Small World, and are cathedrals of imagination.

Moreover there are no chinks in the armour at which cynics like me can sneer – it does what every good piece of theatre should do, suspends one's disbelief. Totally.

If I had to criticise I would mention the crowds and queues which can be oppressive. The merchandising is shamelessly unrelenting and it would be nice to see a vegetable on the menu occasionally.

But overall I would give the whole European Disney experience a qualified thumbs up, partly because it saves us having to go across the Atlantic . . . I would draw the line at making Disney the basis for a family holiday.

I queried the children on this subject.

They looked at me as if I were still trying to speak French. How could I have dragged them off to those unfamiliar distant places, when Disneyland had been right there, under their noses, all the time?

Writing to inform, explain and describe

In your examination you will be given the task of producing a piece of writing that **informs**, **explains** and/or **describes**.

As with any other piece of writing, you will need to take care to write accurately, clearly and in an appropriate style.

However, you also need to practise some of the particular skills associated with writing to inform, explain and/or describe. In this section, we will make clear the difference between these terms, but, as you will discover, there are many similarities and overlap between them. Although the activities you will do focus on each of the three elements separately, in the exam question it is possible that two or more elements will be combined. The specimen papers at the end of this Unit will show how this works in practice.

Writing to inform

When you are writing to inform, your main intention is to convey knowledge about something to someone who wants to find out about that subject. The information may be factual or it may be part of a more imaginative piece of writing. What is important is that you keep two things clear in your mind:

- Who the reader is
- What the reader needs to know.

REMEMBER

When writing to give information you do not need to write a story, use direct speech or use imaginative, descriptive language. Your main concern is to communicate information as clearly as possible.

ACTIVITY 1

Look at the example of informative writing on page 38, taken from a travel guide to Germany.

1 What is the purpose of this writing?
2 Who is the intended audience?
3 How does the writer convey the information clearly?
4 Is there any further information that you would like included?

Facts for the Visitor

PLANNING

When to Go

Any time can be the best time to visit Germany, depending on what you want to do. However, the climate can vary quite a bit according to the location, season and even the year, so it's best to be prepared for all types of weather at all times. The most reliable weather lasts from May to October, coinciding, of course, with the standard tourist season (except for skiing).

The shoulder seasons can bring fewer tourists and surprisingly pleasant weather. In April and May, for instance, flowers and fruit trees are in bloom, and the weather can be surprisingly mild. Indian summers that stretch well into the autumn are not uncommon.

The mean annual temperature in Berlin is 11 °C, the average range of temperatures varying from −1 °C in January to 18 °C in July. The average annual precipitation for all of Germany is 690mm and there is no special rainy season. The camping season generally runs from May to September though some sites open as early as Easter and close in late October or even November.

If you're keen on winter sports, ski resorts, slopes and cross-country trails in the Alps, Harz Mountains and Black Forest begin operating in (usually late) November and move into full swing after the New Year, closing down again when the snows begin to melt in March.

The Climate section and the Climate Charts in the preceding Facts about the Country chapter explain what to expect and when to expect it.

What Kind of Trip?

Go Solo? Travelling alone is not a problem in Germany; the country is well developed and generally safe. Hostels and camping grounds are good places to meet fellow travellers so even if you're travelling alone, you need never be lonely.

The Getting Around chapter has information on organised tours. See also Tourist Offices later in this chapter for a list of German tourist offices abroad.

Move or Stay? 'If this is Tuesday, it must be Munich.' Though often ridiculed, the mad dash that 'does' an entire country the size of Germany in a couple of weeks can have its merits. If you've never visited Germany before, you won't know which areas you'll like, and a quick 'scouting tour' will give an overview of the options. A rail pass that offers unlimited travel within a set period can be the best way to do this.

If you know where you want to go, have found a place you like or have specific interests like hiking or folk culture, the best advice is to stay put for a while, discover some of the lesser known sights, make a few local friends and settle in. It's also cheaper in the long run.

Maps

Locally produced maps of Germany are among the best in the world. Most tourist offices distribute free (but very basic) city maps. Two auto associations, Allgemeiner Deutscher Automobil Club (ADAC) and Automobilclub von Deutschland (AvD), produce excellent road maps.

What to Bring

Take along as little as possible; if you forget to bring it, you can buy it in Germany.

In general, standard dress in Germany is very casual, but fairly conservative outside the largest cities. Jeans are generally accepted throughout the country though denim and trainers (sneakers) are banned at certain up-market discos. Men needn't bother bringing a necktie; it will seldom – if ever – be used except maybe at certain casinos. Layers of clothing are best, as weather can change drastically from region to region and from day to night.

If you plan to stay at hostels, pack or buy a towel and a plastic soap container when you arrive. Bedclothes are almost always provided, though you might want to take along your own sheet bag. You'll sleep easier with a padlock on one of the storage lockers usually provided at hostels.

Other items you might need include a torch (flashlight), an adapter plug for electrical appliances (such as a cup or coil immersion heater to make your own tea or instant coffee), a universal bath/sink plug (a plastic film canister sometimes works), sunglasses, a few clothes pegs and premoistened towelettes or a large cotton handkerchief that you can soak in fountains and use to cool off while touring cities and towns in the warmer months.

From *The Lonely Planet Guide to Germany* by Anthony Haywood

ACTIVITY 2

Re-read the extract from the travel guide carefully and then write a brief letter
to a friend who will shortly be taking a holiday in Germany with his/her family
telling him/her of the main things to prepare for.

ACTIVITY 3

Now read the extract below.

1 Describe how it is different from the travel guide on page 38.

2 What differences do you notice about the writer's approach and use of language?

For forty-two years, Lewis and Benjamin Jones slept side by side, in their parents' bed, at their farm
which was known as 'The Vision'.

The bedstead, an oak four-poster, came from their mother's home at Bryn-Draenog when she
married in 1899. Its faded cretonne hangings, printed with a design of larkspur and roses, shut out the
mosquitoes of summer, and the draughts in winter. Calloused heels had worn holes in the linen sheets,
and parts of the patchwork quilt had frayed. Under the goose-feather mattress, there was a second
mattress, of horsehair, and this had sunk into two troughs, leaving a ridge between the sleepers.

The room was always dark and smelled of lavender and mothballs.

The smell of mothballs came from a pyramid of hatboxes piled up beside the washstand. On the bed-
table lay a pin-cushion still stuck with Mrs Jones's hatpins; and on the end wall hung an engraving of
Holman Hunt's 'Light of the World', enclosed in an ebonized frame.

One of the windows looked out over the green fields of England: the other looked back into Wales,
past a clump of larches, at the Black Hill …

The house had roughcast walls and a roof of mossy stone tiles and stood at the far end of the farmyard
in the shade of an old Scots pine. Below the cowshed there was an orchard of wind-stunted apple-trees,
and then the fields slanted down to the dingle, and there were birches and alders along the stream.

Long ago, the place had been called Ty-Cradoc – and Caractacus is still a name in these parts – but
in 1737 an ailing girl called Alice Morgan saw the Virgin hovering over a patch of rhubarb, and ran back
to the kitchen, cured. To celebrate the miracle, her father renamed his farm 'The Vision' and carved the
initials A.M. with the date and a cross on the lintel above the porch. The border of Radnor and
Hereford was said to run right through the middle of the staircase.

The brothers were identical twins.

As boys, only their mother could tell them apart: now age and accidents had weathered them in
different ways.

Lewis was tall and stringy, with shoulders set square and a steady long-limbed stride. Even at eighty
he could walk over the hills all day, or wield an axe all day, and not get tired.

He gave off a strong smell. His eyes – grey, dreamy and astygmatic – were set well back into the
skull, and capped with thick round lenses in white metal frames. He bore the scar of a cycling accident
on his nose and, ever since, its tip had curved downwards and turned purple in cold weather.

His head would wobble as he spoke: unless he was fumbling with his watch-chain, he had no idea what
to do with his hands. In company he always wore a puzzled look; and if anyone made a statement of fact,
he'd say, 'Thank you!' or 'Very kind of you!' Everyone agreed he had a wonderful way with sheepdogs.

Benjamin was shorter, pinker, neater and sharper-tongued. His chin fell into his neck, but he still
possessed the full stretch of his nose, which he would use in conversation as a weapon. He had less hair.

He did all the cooking, the darning and the ironing; and he kept the accounts. No one could be
fiercer in a haggle over stock-prices and he would go on, arguing for hours, until the dealer threw up
his hands and said, 'Come off, you old skinflint!' and he'd smile and say, 'What can you mean by that?'

For miles around the twins had the reputation of being incredibly stingy – but this was not always so.

From On the Black Hill by Bruce Chatwin

 **ACTIVITY 4**

The extract on page 39 is the opening of a novel. The author is providing us with information about two of the main characters.

Write three or four paragraphs in which you explain how the writer conveys this information particularly through his use of language. Consider:

● the descriptions of Lewis and Benjamin

● the house in which they live and its furniture

● the views from the house's windows.

KEY POINTS

Although the writers of the two pieces on pages 38 and 39 have entirely different purposes, their approach is similar. Both pieces of information are:

🔑 expressed clearly with carefully chosen vocabulary

🔑 ordered and structured   🔑 detailed and well developed.

 **ACTIVITY 5**

Your family is exchanging houses with a family from the United States as part of their holiday arrangements. The visiting family has a daughter of your age. Write an information guide for her in which you:

1 tell her about your house and the room that she will be using

2 provide her with information about the facilities available in your area.

Plan your work

This is a fairly straightforward task. It needs a clear and structured plan. Remember, it is a good idea to decide on your audience before you start to write. After all, although it's easiest to keep details of the house and area mainly factual, you have the freedom to decide what sort of a person you are writing for, what her interests might be and how familiar she is with the way of life in the UK.

You could organise your answer using the following plan.

Paragraph 1	Describe your room: storage space; any things of interest you have left; how to use TV, CD player, etc. Draw attention to any particular problems – creaking radiators, doors that don't shut.
Paragraph 2	Give information about the house: where it is; how to get into town (buses, etc.); garden; any things your parents would expect to be carefully looked after.
Paragraph 3	Describe facilities in the area: places of entertainment (cinemas; nightclubs; discos; theatres); particular features (seaside; country walks); places to avoid.

Writing to explain

Although writing to explain also requires you to use a reasonably formal register, it needs a slightly different approach from writing to inform. Again, you will need to have some knowledge of *what* you are writing about but instead of just telling your audience about it, you need to explain *how* things are done or occur.

ACTIVITY 6

Look at the texts below and on page 42. Copy the table below and make notes on the questions for each text.

Questions	Text 1	Text 2
What is being explained?		
Describe the register being used.		
Who is the intended audience?		
What have you learned?		

Text 1

How a lens gathers light

Light travels in straight lines until it encounters a solid object; and air, glass, water, people, metal – in fact anything that can be seen – are all more or less 'solid' in that light cannot pass straight through them unimpeded. On meeting one of these substances light may be redirected (by reflection and/or refraction) or absorbed. In practice both usually happen together, but in what proportions depends on the properties of the surface.

All surfaces except matt black ones reflect at least some of the light that falls on them and absorb the rest. It is the quantity and spectral composition of the light they reflect that gives them their distinguishing characteristics: according to quantity we call a surface dull or bright; according to its spectral composition we attribute a colour to it, and these are the factors that give what we perceive as form, substance and colour to the physical world.

When light strikes any point of a matt surface its reflected component explodes off in many directions at once (which is how it becomes 'visible' from all around) so that an environment cluttered with objects of all shapes, sizes and colours – e.g. the earth's surface – is constantly bombarded with light of all densities and qualities, from every direction, reflected and re-reflected in a turbulent but highly organized bedlam of visual sensations – like millions upon millions of people all furiously playing ping-pong on the same small table.

The lens of a camera, like that of the eye, receives over its entire surface light emanating from every point in the world before it. As the rays from any given point pass through the lens they are refracted, or bent, so that instead of continuing to spread out they converge again, finally coming to a point, or 'focus' on the other side. As long as the photographic film is situated in the plane of focus a precise image of the subject will be formed on the film when the exposure is made.

From Pentax ME Super Book of Photography

Text 2

When you have been down in two or three pits you begin to get some grasp of the processes that are going on underground. (I ought to say, by the way, that I know nothing whatever about the technical side of mining: I am merely describing what I have seen.) Coal lies in thin seams between enormous layers of rock, so that essentially the process of getting it out is like scooping the central layer from a Neapolitan ice. In the old days the miners used to cut straight into the coal with pick and crowbar – a very slow job because coal, when lying in its virgin state, is almost as hard as rock. Nowadays the preliminary work is done by an electrically-driven coal-cutter, which in principle is an immensely tough and powerful band-saw, running horizontally instead of vertically, with teeth a couple of inches long and half an inch or an inch thick. It can move backwards or forwards on its own power, and the men operating it can rotate it this way or that. Incidentally it makes one of the most awful noises I have ever heard, and sends forth clouds of coal dust which make it impossible to see more than two to three feet and almost impossible to breathe. The machine travels along the coal face cutting into the base of the coal and undermining it to the depth of five feet or five feet and a half; after this it is comparatively easy to extract the coal to the depth to which it has been undermined. Where it is 'difficult getting', however, it has also to be loosened with explosives. A man with an electric drill, like a rather small version of the drills used in street-mending, bores holes at intervals in the coal, inserts blasting powder, plugs it with clay, goes round the corner if there is one handy (he is supposed to retire to twenty-five yards distance) and touches off the charge with an electric current. This is not intended to bring the coal out, only to loosen it. Occasionally, of course, the charge is too powerful, and then it not only brings the coal out but brings the roof down as well.

After the blasting has been done the 'fillers' can tumble the coal out, break it up and shovel it on to the conveyor belt. It comes out first in monstrous boulders which may weigh anything up to twenty tons. The conveyor belt shoots it on to tubs, and the tubs are shoved into the main road and hitched on to an endlessly revolving steel cable which drags them to the cage. Then they are hoisted, and at the surface the coal is sorted by being run over screens, and if necessary is washed as well. As far as possible the 'dirt' – the shale, that is – is used for making the roads below. All that cannot be used is sent to the surface and dumped; hence the monstrous 'dirt-heaps', like hideous grey mountains, which are the characteristic scenery of the coal areas. When the coal has been extracted to the depth to which the machine has cut, the coal face has advanced by five feet. Fresh props are put in to hold up the newly exposed roof, and during the next shift the conveyor belt is taken to pieces, moved five feet forward and re-assembled. As far as possible the three operations of cutting, blasting and extraction are done in three separate shifts, the cutting in the afternoon, the blasting at night (there is a law, not always kept, that forbids its being done when other men are working near by), and the 'filling' in the morning shift, which lasts from six in the morning until half past one.

Even when you watch the process of coal-extraction you probably only watch it for a short time, and it is not until you begin making a few calculations that you realize what a stupendous task the 'fillers' are performing. Normally each man has to clear a space four or five yards wide. The cutter has undermined the coal to the depth of five feet, so that if the seam of coal is three or four feet high, each man has to cut out, break up and load on to the belt something between seven and twelve cubic yards of coal. This is to say, taking a cubic yard as weighing twenty-seven hundred-weight, that each man is shifting coal at a speed approaching two tons an hour. I have just enough experience of pick and shovel work to be able to grasp what this means. When I am digging trenches in my garden, if I shift two tons of earth during the afternoon, I feel that I have earned my tea. But earth is tractable stuff compared with coal, and I don't have to work kneeling down, a thousand feet underground, in suffocating heat and swallowing coal dust with every breath I take; nor do I have to walk a mile bent double before I begin. The miner's job would be as much beyond my power as it would be to perform on a flying trapeze or to win the Grand National. I am not a manual labourer and please God I never shall be one, but there are some kinds of manual work that I could do if I had to. At a pitch I could be a tolerable road-sweeper or an inefficient gardener or even a tenth-rate farm hand. But by no conceivable amount of effort or training could I become a coal-miner; the work would kill me in a few weeks.

From *Down the Mine* by George Orwell

Text 1 is from a textbook and is aimed at a certain audience who are likely to be interested in the subject matter and wish to know more about it to further their expertise in photography. Text 2 is of more general interest.

Although both texts are good examples of writing to explain, Orwell's might be the better model to use for an examination task.

ACTIVITY 7

Using your notes from Activity 6 about 'What is being explained?', rewrite Text 2 as a technical piece of explanation in the style of Text 1.

KEY POINTS

 Try to get inside the heads of your readers. What *you* understand clearly and take for granted, *they* may need to have explained in considerable detail.

Use technical vocabulary, an objective, impersonal tone and diagrams to help make the point clear.

A more personal approach, using the personal pronoun 'you' and using personal references, helps the reader relate to what is being explained.

The more personal approach, vocabulary and similes can prevent overload of technical vocabulary.

Some useful words and phrases for this section

Action verbs	Present tense	General pronouns	Connectives

You can make your writing for this section effective by:

- addressing the reader in a general way: *you, people,* etc.
- using the simple present tense: *You do this by* ...
- using mainly action verbs (at the start of sentences):

  Follow these instructions ...   *Plan your work carefully* ...

- using connectives to do with time or cause and effect to link sentences and paragraphs, such as: *next, then, after, owing to, as a result of this.*

 ACTIVITY 8

Write an article for a school magazine in which you explain how to take part in a particular sport or leisure activity and why you find this particular activity enjoyable. Choose an activity with which you are familiar. Include details about:

- what the activity involves
- equipment needed
- where you can take part in it
- costs to be incurred
- what you find enjoyable and why it might appeal to your readers.

 REMEMBER

Every time you make a particular point ask yourself the question: 'Why have I said that?' Your next sentence should be the answer to that question.

Writing to describe

When you are writing to describe, you are trying to recreate for the reader your impressions of something or someone. In order to do this convincingly, you need to picture details clearly and sharply in your own mind before you start to write.

Look at the three texts below and on pages 45–46. The first one describes a place, the second an object and the third a person. The subject matter made a strong impression on the writer in each case.

Text 1

My presents having been duly inspected and the family thanked, I then went round to the back veranda with Leslie, and there lay a mysterious shape covered with a tarpaulin. Leslie drew this aside with the air of a conjuror, and there lay my boat. I gazed at it rapturously; it was surely the most perfect boat that anyone had ever had. Gleaming in her coat of new paint she lay there, my steed to the enchanted archipelago.

The boat was some seven feet long, and almost circular in shape. Leslie explained hurriedly – in case I thought the shape was due to defective craftsmanship – that the reason for this was that the planks had been too short for the frame, an explanation I found perfectly satisfactory. After all, it was the sort of irritating thing that could have happened to anyone. I said stoutly that I thought it was a lovely shape for a boat, and indeed I thought it was. She was not sleek, slim, and rather predatory looking, like most boats, but rotund, placid, and somehow comforting in her circular solidarity. She reminded me of an earnest dungbeetle, an insect for which I had great affection. Leslie, pleased at my evident delight, said deprecatingly that he had been forced to make her flat-bottomed, since, for a variety of technical reasons, this was the safest. I said that I liked flat-bottomed boats the best, because it was possible to put jars of specimens on the floor without so much risk of them upsetting. Leslie asked me if I liked the colour scheme, as he had not been too sure about it. Now, in my opinion, the colour scheme was the best thing about it, the final touch that completed the unique craft. Inside she was painted green and white, while her bulging sides were tastefully covered in white, black, and brilliant orange stripes, a combination of colours that struck me as being both artistic and friendly. Leslie then showed me the long, smooth cypress pole he had cut for a mast, but explained that it could not be fitted into position until the boat was launched. Enthusiastically I suggested launching her at once. Leslie, who was a stickler for procedure, said you couldn't launch a ship without naming her, and had I thought of a name yet? This was a difficult problem, and the whole family were called out to help me solve it. They stood clustered round the boat, which looked like a gigantic flower in their midst, and racked their brains.

'Why not call it the *Jolly Roger*?' suggested Margo.

I rejected this scornfully; I explained that I wanted a sort of *fat* name that would go with the boat's appearance and personality.

'*Arburckle*,' suggested Mother vaguely.

That was no use, either; the boat simply didn't look like an Arbuckle.

'Call it the *Ark*,' said Leslie, but I shook my head.

From *My Family and Other Animals* by Gerald Durrell

Text 2

Great Uncle Arthur was a stunted and bandy man, with a dark, sallow and strong boned face. He looked very yellow. He had a heavy head of wiry hair as black as coals, ragged eyebrows and a horrible long black beard like a crinkled mat of pubic hair. A reek of tobacco, varnish and wood-shavings came off him; he had large fingers with split unclean nails. The first thing he did when he got home from work was to put on a white apron, strap a pair of carpet knee-pads to his trousers, pick up a hammer or screw-driver and start on odd jobs round the house. He was always hammering something and was often up a ladder. His great yellow teeth gave me the idea he had a machine of some kind in his mouth, and that they were fit to bite nails; in fact, he often pulled a nail or two out of his mouth. He seemed to chew them.

Uncle Arthur's wife was Grandma's eldest sister and in every way unlike her. She was tall, big boned, very white faced and hollow-eyed and had large, loose, laughing teeth like a horse's or a skeleton's which have ever since seemed to me the signs of hilarious good nature in a woman. Though she looked ill – breathing those fumes of the gas works which filled the house cannot have been very good for her – she was jolly, hard-working and affectionate. She and Uncle Arthur were notorious (in the family) for the incredible folly of adoring each other. She doted on her dark, scowling, argumentative, hammering little gnome: it seemed that two extraordinary sets of teeth had fallen in love with each other.

For myself, Uncle Arthur's parlour, Aunt Sarah's kitchen and the small back yard were the attractions. The back yard was only a few feet square but he grew calceolarias there. It gave on to an alley, one wall of which was part of the encircling wall of the city. Its 'Bars' or city gates, its Minster are the grandest in England and to Uncle Arthur who knew every stone in the place I owe my knowledge and love of it. One could go up the steps, only a few feet and walk along the battlements and shoot imaginary arrows from the very spot where the Yorkists had shot them in the Wars of the Roses; and one could look down on the white roses of York in the gardens near the Minster and look up to those towers where the deep bells talked out their phenomenal words over the roofs of the city. They moved me then; they move me still.

Uncle Arthur's house had a stuffy smell – the smell of the gas works and the railway beyond it was mixed with the odour of camphor and camphor wax. The rooms were poorly lit by gas jets burning under grubby white globes; air did not move easily, for there were heavy curtains in the narrow passage-way to the stairs. But the pinched little place contained Uncle's genius and the smell of camphor indicated it. The cabinet-maker was a naturalist – he used to speak of Nature as some loud fancy woman he went about with and whom his wife had got used to.

From A Cab at the Door by V. S. Pritchett

45

Text 3

It was nearly dusk. A couple of hundred yards further on the path rounded a bend through the trees and ended suddenly, breathtakingly, in a viewing platform hanging out over a precipice of rock – a little patio in the sky. It was a look-out built for the public, but I had the feeling that no one had been there for years, certainly no tourist. It was the sheerest stroke of luck that I had stumbled on it. I had never seen anything half as beautiful: on one side the town of Capri spilling down the hillside, on the other the twinkling lights of the cove at Anacapri and the houses gathered around it, and in front of me a sheer drop of – what? – 200 feet, 300 feet, to a sea of the lushest aquamarine washing against outcrops of jagged rock. The sea was so far below that the sound of breaking waves reached me as the faintest of whispers. A sliver of moon, brilliantly white, hung in a pale blue evening sky, a warm breeze teased my hair and everywhere there was the scent of lemon, honeysuckle and pine. It was like being in the household-products section of Sainsbury's. Ahead of me there was nothing but open sea, calm and seductive, for 150 miles to Sicily. I would do anything to own that view, anything. ...

Just above me, I realised after a moment, overlooking this secret place was the patio of a villa set back just out of sight. Somebody *did* own that view, could sit there every morning with his muesli and orange juice, in his Yves St Laurent bathrobe and Gucci slippers, and look out on this sweep of Mediterranean heaven.

From *Neither Here Nor There* by Bill Bryson

ACTIVITY 9

Read all three texts carefully. Think about how well the writers have succeeded in conveying their feelings and impressions to you. In particular, consider their choice of vocabulary, the similes and metaphors they use and their tone of voice. For each text, make a list of the words and phrases that:

- contain clear and vivid descriptions
- convey the writer's feelings and attitude.

ACTIVITY 10

Now look at each text separately and answer the following questions.

Text 1

Gerald Durrell describes a boat that his brother, Leslie, made him for a birthday present when he was a young boy. There is a considerable amount of affectionate humour in the description.

1 Comment on the effect of the following expressions.

- 'Leslie explained ... that the planks had been too short for the frame'
- 'She was not sleek, slim, and rather predatory looking, like most boats'
- 'She reminded me of an earnest dungbeetle'
- '... her bulging sides were tastefully covered in white, black, and brilliant orange stripes'

2 Why do you think that 'rotund' is a better word to describe the boat than 'fat' or 'round'?

How does the writer convey a sense of childhood happiness?

Text 2

What do you think the writer's feelings were towards Uncle Arthur and Aunt Sarah? In your answer, refer in detail to the way in which he describes these characters and the house in which they lived.

Text 3

1 What exactly did Bill Bryson find so impressive about the view?

2 Why do you think it affected him in this way?

3 Think up some words to describe what he felt about the view and the mood he was in.

4 Find quotations from the extract that illustrate the words you have chosen, giving reasons.

KEY POINTS

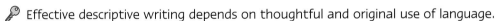 Effective descriptive writing depends on thoughtful and original use of language.

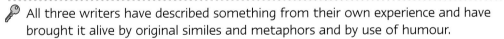 All three writers have described something from their own experience and have brought it alive by original similes and metaphors and by use of humour.

 The reader is interested and kept alert by the writing.

ACTIVITY 11

Write a description of yourself and members of your family as you think your neighbours would see you.

This allows you quite a free hand. You are able to write about some people with whom you are very familiar but to do so from a slightly unusual perspective. You do not, of course, have to worry too much as to whether what you write is really what your neighbours think. Remember to use original and lively comparisons; the topic provides you with the opportunity to attempt some humour. You could try a really different perspective and describe your family from the point of view of the neighbour's pet dog or cat!

Exam practice

How to approach Section A

Section A tests your reading skills. You will need to show that you understand what you have read and appreciate the techniques used by different writers to convey their information and opinions to you. It involves the reading of non-fiction and media texts of the types we have looked at in this Unit.

 REMEMBER

+ You should read the questions just as carefully as you read the texts themselves.
+ Some questions ask you to show *what* you have understood, others ask you to explain *how* something is done. Don't confuse the two.

Some words of advice

You will have about 1 hour to answer the questions in this section. You can afford to spend at least 20 minutes of that hour in reading and note making. Once you know what you intend to write, it does not take long to write the words on the paper. You may find the following approach helpful.

> **Read through all the questions carefully. Underline or highlight key words.**

> **Read through the texts on which the questions are set. Don't skip over difficult sections. Think of the questions your teacher would ask you in lessons and ask yourself the same questions in your mind.**

> **Look for implied as well as specific points.**

> **Underline or highlight parts of the text relevant to the task. Are they facts or opinions?**

> **Think about the writer's audience and purpose.**

> **Make notes to organise your answer. Use your own words as far as possible.**

> **Now you're ready to write your final version.**

How to approach Section B

 REMEMBER

Section B tests your skills in writing to inform, explain and/or describe. Although we have looked at these areas separately in this Unit, in the exam question it is possible that they will be combined. What is important is that in your writing you use a suitable register for the task.

Some words of advice

You will have about 45–50 minutes to answer this question. There will be no choice of task but the reading material in Section A may help to give you some ideas as a starting point for what you are going to write about.

> **Read the task carefully. Does it require you to inform, explain and/or describe or is it a combination of these approaches?**

> **Spend some time planning what you are going to write although you will not have time to write an over-elaborate plan.**

> **Don't plan to write too much. 400-450 words will be adequate. That means about 6-8 well-developed paragraphs.**

> **The main points in your plan (once you've put them in the best order) will provide topic sentences for your paragraphs. Remember that a well-focused introduction and a planned conclusion will help your reader to follow your ideas easily.**

> **Think carefully about the context of the task; for example, you could be asked to write a magazine article, a note containing instructions for a friend, a formal letter or even the words of a talk that you might give.**

> **Decide on an appropriate register to use – you will be given credit for showing awareness of this. Establish the register clearly in your opening paragraph.**

> **Now you are ready to start to write.**

> **Remember to leave yourself time to check through your writing at the end.**

Practice paper: Foundation Tier

SECTION A

Non-fiction texts

1 Read carefully the **two** texts below and on page 51 about teenage drinking and then write **one paragraph on each** of the following:

   a the reasons why doctors and other people think that heavy drinking by young teenagers is dangerous

   b the suggestions as to what can be done to reduce these dangers.

   You should write about **150–200 words in total**. Remember to use your own words as far as possible.

2 Using both the facts and other information given in the texts explain why people are concerned about the way alcohol is being marketed to the young.

Text 1

Industry Targets the Young

'Scandal as drink bosses target our children' was the headline in the Daily Express. The article was inspired by the recent Eurocare publication, 'Marketing Alcohol to Young People', an eye-catching brochure which brings together examples of advertisements from all over the world. The text shows how the drink industry cynically sets out to persuade the young to consume alcohol by making it appear glamorous, fashionable, and amusing. The advertisements associate alcohol with sporting and sexual prowess. Heroes of the football field play with the logo of a particular beer emblazoned across their chests. Beautiful young women imply a willingness to surrender to the man who swills a particular kind of booze. Perhaps most notoriously, there is the Carlsberg baby – a child of a few months who, in the colours of Liverpool FC, is already a living advertisement for Carlsberg lager.

   It was this last image which caught the attention of Gro Harlem Brundtland, the Director General of the World Health Organisation, at the recent ministerial meeting in Stockholm on Young People and Alcohol. Holding up the brochure, she said that this was evidence of what governments concerned about the well-being of youth were up against.

   Besides the Daily Express, other major national newspapers took up the story, as did television and radio.

The industry was perhaps unprepared and could only come up with the comment that 'Marketing Alcohol to Young People' was 'inaccurate and misleading' though the various spokesmen could hardly deny that the advertisements were genuine and spoke for themselves. 'Self-regulation is working,' said the industry's Portman Group and it is true that a number of complaints have been upheld but these have been against such flagrant violations that they could hardly be ignored without the system being totally discredited. Those working with the problem would say that what is much more insidious is the relentless pressure exerted by the kind of advertising strategies highlighted in 'Marketing Alcohol to Young People'. The fact is that problems arising from alcohol use among the young are rising, particularly in the United Kingdom, and there is a vast consequent cost to the NHS – besides the terrible personal price many families have to pay. At least the Portman Group is happy with how things are going on the self-regulation front.

   Ironically on the day 'Marketing Alcohol to Young People' was reported in The Daily Telegraph, the same newspaper announced a 'ground-breaking' appointment at Bacardi-Martini, one of the Portman Group's major funders: a marketing director with special responsibility for 'the youth market' and audiences at musical events.

Text 2

News Online: Health

Teenage drinking

Doctors are worried about an apparent increase in the number of young teenagers who are drinking heavily.

While many of the more serious health effects of drinking affect those who have been drinking for many years, it is feared that alcohol abuse during the formative years sets a pattern for later life.

The British Medical Association (BMA) published a report highlighting these fears last year.

'Alcohol and Young People' suggested that not only was there a general rise in the proportion of 11 to 15-year-olds who drink alcohol regularly, but also that there is an increase in the amount they are drinking on each occasion.

Alcohol Concern suggested that a third more 11–15 year olds are drinking regularly.

It is far easier to work out the health effects of drinking on adults – it is known that heavy drinking over the years is a risk factor for certain cancers, particularly oral and liver, and raised blood pressure which can contribute to heart disease.

'Binge' drinking every now and then tends to be far more harmful to health than drinking a moderate amount occasionally.

It has also been suggested that teenagers are more likely to have casual sex if they are regular drinkers.

Harming the young

Doctors think that this effect could be far more pronounced in the young, as alcohol will tend to have more effect on their developing bodies.

The increase in the availability of 'designer drinks', the so-called 'alcopops' has been accused of making alcohol far more attractive to younger people.

Research has shown that it is particularly the 13–16 age group that is attracted to the idea of alcopops.

A spokesman for the BMA said: 'There is a need for government action to address the problems of underage and teenage drinking.

'This must involve changes to legislation, responsible marketing, effective monitoring of the drinks industry and health education.'

In Scotland, it is an offence for anyone under 18 to buy alcohol for a person under 18 years old – the BMA would like to see that legislation introduced in England and Wales.

It also called for:

- Tougher regulation of advertising for alcoholic drinks by the Independent Television Commission and the Advertising Standards Authority

- The creation of an independent regulator with powers of enforcement to review complaints about marketing practices

- More spot-checks on retailers using 'test purchases' by under-18s

- Extension of current voluntary proof-of-age ID schemes

- More alcohol education to be introduced from primary school level

The Portman Group, which sets standards for advertising within the alcohol industry, has taken steps to prevent it appealing to young teenagers.

This week, it announced a ban on the use of words such as 'revitalising' in connection with drinks which contain a stimulant such as caffeine as well as alcohol.

Media text

3 The writer of the booklet reproduced below and opposite is trying to warn readers of the dangers of under-age drinking and to advise how to avoid them. Read the text carefully.

Consider how information is presented in this booklet. Refer to three or four examples and say why you have chosen them.

In your answer you could write about:

- how the writer's use of **words and phrases** help to convey the writer's advice
- how the type of **information** the writer provides helps to convey his advice.

 A Laugh

We all like a laugh. And you can't have a laugh on a night out without having a bit of a drink, can you? After all, what's the point of going out if you're not going to have a drink or several to keep up with your mates?

The trouble with alcohol is there's no off-switch, no going-back.

You want to feel good so you keep drinking. If you're with a group, you're probably drinking rounds. You're drinking quickly. Too quickly to keep track of how many. Before you know it, you've had way too much and feel really rough. So you have another drink, hoping you'll get back to feeling good. Soon you don't feel anything at all.

Except when you wake up the next day and can't remember how you got there or what you did. *And that's scary.*

If you're in your early teens or younger, there's more bad news ...

Your body isn't fully grown so alcohol will affect you quicker than an adult. You might feel sick, take stupid risks, lose control and even blackout by drinking a lot less than someone older.

1,000 young people under 15 are admitted to hospital each year with acute alcohol poisoning. All need emergency treatment.

It's stupid to try and drink at the same level as adults or some of your older friends. Getting drunk won't make you one of their crowd. They'll be laughing at you not with you. Alcohol has been around for thousands of years. It'll still be there when you're older.

Drink for drink, alcohol will also have more effect on a woman than a man. It's a biological fact. Women are generally smaller, their bodies contain less water and their metabolism is different.

Drinking alcohol together with taking drugs is especially dangerous, increasing the likelihood of serious overdose.

cons of getting canned continued ...

- Around half of all pedestrians aged 16–60 killed in road accidents have more booze in their bloodstream than the legal drink–drive limit.

- Around half of all adults admitted to hospital with head injuries are drunk.

- Alcohol's a factor in at least seven per cent of accidental drownings and 40% of household fires.

- You can get a criminal record for offences of drunkenness. Being drunk will be no excuse if you end up in court on a charge of criminal damage or violence.

- Getting drunk may mean you end up doing something you regret. Like getting off with Mr or Miss Personality Bypass. Or having sex when you don't really want to. Or not bothering to use a condom and risking getting a sexually transmitted disease.

Still feeling good about getting trashed?

SECTION B

Writing to inform, explain, describe

Write an article for a school magazine aimed at students in Year 7, informing them of some of the problems they may face in their social lives as they go through the school and describing the help they can get in coping with them.

Reviewing your paper

Section A Question 1

Question 1a asks you to read the passages and write about the reasons why doctors and other people are worried about the increase in teenage drinking.

What do you need to do?

You are being asked to select material containing *reasons*. That means you must say *why* something is so.

The first point is to be found in Text 2, paragraph two: '... it is feared that alcohol abuse during the formative years sets a pattern for later life'. You could show an understanding of this in your own words in the following way:

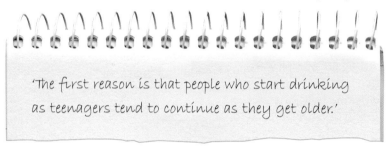

'The first reason is that people who start drinking as teenagers tend to continue as they get older.'

List the further points that you find, but remember that you must put them into your own words when writing your final version. The first two appropriate points would be:

- Doctors and others are worried about the amount young teenagers are drinking.
- This may result in the teenagers continuing to drink heavily as they grow older.

Question 1b asks you to identify the suggestions as to what can be done to reduce teenage drinking.

What do you need to do?

Select points about suggested ways to deal with the problem. Many of these can be found at the end of the second text. However, to answer this task well, you will need to express the points in your own words and collate them together. For example, the sentence beginning 'This must involve changes to legislation ...' could be started in this way:

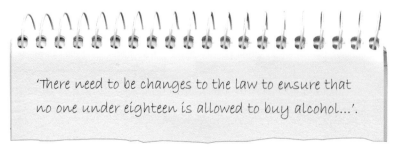

'There need to be changes to the law to ensure that no one under eighteen is allowed to buy alcohol...'.

Identify other relevant points and then explain them in the same way.

Section A Question 2

Question 2 asks you to use *facts* and *information* from the texts to explain why people are concerned about the ways alcohol is being marketed to the young.

What do you need to do?

If you read the question carefully, the purpose of the task is clearly identified. Use this writing frame as a basis for your answer.

Structure	Content
Paragraph 1	There are various reasons why people are concerned about the way alcohol is being marketed to the young.
Paragraph 2	One reason is that young teenagers are led to believe that bingeing on alcopops is part of a glamorous and exciting lifestyle.
Paragraph 3	This causes concern because …
Paragraph 4	Other reasons for concern include the ways in which alcohol is being advertised.
Paragraph 5	This is particularly worrying because …
Paragraph 6	These are the main reasons but there are other concerns as well such as …

Section A Question 3

Question 3 is based on a media text and requires you to explain the ways in which the text attempts to warn and advise readers about the dangers of under-age drinking, in particular by looking at the way it presents information.

What do you need to do?

The question contains bullet points to help you focus your answer. Make good use of them. This is a *how* question. Remember to explain why you have chosen the statements you have quoted.

You could start by quoting the following:

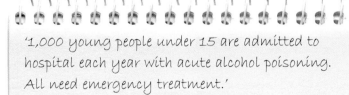

'1,000 young people under 15 are admitted to hospital each year with acute alcohol poisoning. All need emergency treatment.'

A comment on this might include the following points.

- This is a factual statement.
- Printed in bold type.
- Expressed as a single paragraph.
- Short, direct second sentence conveys a blunt warning statement.
- More friendly tone of the next paragraph 'It's stupid'.
- This gives suitable register for target audience.

Now identify three more statements and explain how effectively you think they are presented. In particular, you could look at the way the writer has used quotations.

Section B

The writing task asks you to *inform* and *describe*. You are given a specific purpose and audience for your writing.

What do you need to do?

Try to use a register suited to Year 7 students.

Plan your work carefully. Think of the problems you and your friends encountered during your earlier years at school. Use these as a basis for your writing. Don't include too many points, but explain fully those that you do make.

Good responses

✔ use correct spelling, punctuation and well-structured paragraphs

✔ show positive merit of vocabulary

✔ use a range of sentence structures

✔ show clear awareness of audience and purpose.

Practice paper: Higher Tier

Non-fiction text

The Guardian Thursday June 21, 2001

Comment

Soon all our foods will be polluted by genetic modification

When choice becomes just a memory

Naomi Klein

Europeans would be forgiven for thinking that the war against genetic tampering in the food supply has been all but won. There are labels in the supermarkets aisles, there is mounting political support for organic farming, and Greenpeace campaigners are seen to represent such a mainstream point of view that the courts have let them off for uprooting genetically modified crops. With 35 countries worldwide that have, or are developing, mandatory GM labelling laws, you'd think that the North American agricultural export industry would have no choice but to bow to the demand: keep GM seeds far away from their unaltered counterparts and, in general, move away from the controversial crops.

You'd be wrong. The real strategy is to introduce so much genetic pollution that meeting the consumer demand for GM-free food is seen as not possible. The idea, quite simply, is to pollute faster than countries can legislate – then change the laws to fit the contamination.

A few reports from the front lines of this invisible war. In April, Monsanto recalled about 10% of the GM oilseed rape seeds it had distributed in Canada because of reports that the seeds had been contaminated by another modified rape-seed variety, one not approved for export. The most well-known of these cases is StarLink corn. The genetically altered crop (meant for animals and deemed unfit for humans) made its way into much of the US corn supply after the buffer zones surrounding the fields where it was grown proved wholly incapable of containing the wind-borne pollen. Aventis, which owns the StarLink patent, proposed a solution: instead of recalling the corn, why not approve its consumption for humans?

And there is the now famous case of Percy Schmeiser, the Saskatchewan farmer who was sued by Monsanto after its genetically altered oilseed rape seeds allegedly blew into his field from passing trucks and neighbouring fields. Monsanto says that when the seeds took root, Mr Schmeiser was stealing its property. The court agreed and, two months ago, ordered the farmer to pay the company $20,000, plus legal costs.

Arran Stephens, president of Nature's Path, an organic food company in British Columbia, told the New York Times earlier this month that GM material is even finding its way into organic crops. 'We have found traces in corn that has been grown organically for 10 to 15 years. There's no wall high enough to keep that stuff contained.' Indeed, there is so much genetic contamination in North American fields that a group of organic farmers is considering launching a class action suit against the biotech industry for lost revenues. Last week, the grounds for this case received a significant boost. Loblaws, Canada's largest supermarket chain with 40% of the market, sent out a letter to all of its health food suppliers informing them that they were no longer permitted to claim that their foods were 'non-GM'. Company executives argue there is just no way of knowing what is genuinely GM free.

You can already see the handiwork in the aisles of Canada's major supermarkets: hand-drawn black scribbles on boxes of organic breakfast cereal where the labels used to be. At first glance, Loblaws' decision doesn't seem to make market sense. Although roughly 70% of foods sold in Canada contain GM ingredients, more than 90% of Canadians tell pollsters they want labels telling them if their food's genetic make-up has been tampered with.

In North America, supermarkets are part of a broader agricultural strategy to present labelling as simply too complicated. In part this is because chains like Loblaws are not only food retailers but manufacturers of their own private lines. Loblaws' line is called 'President's Choice' or 'Memories of ...'. Company chairman Galen Weston has warned that 'there will be a cost associated' with labelling and if Loblaws sells some products that are labelled 'GM-free' it weakens attempts to block GM labelling for the rest of its wares.

What does all this mean to Europeans? It means that your labels could soon be as obsolete as the scratched-out ones in our supermarkets. If contamination continues to spread in North America, and agribusiness's current push to overturn Brazil's ban on GM seeds is successful, it will become next to impossible to import non-GM soybeans. Backed by predatory intellectual property laws, agribusinesses are on their way to getting the global food supply so hopelessly cross pollinated, polluted and generally mixed up, that legislators may well be forced to throw up their hands.

When we look back on this moment, munching our genetically modified health-style food, we may well remember it as the precise turning point when we lost our real food options. Perhaps Loblaws will even launch a new product to bottle that wistful feeling: Memories of Consumer Choice.

SECTION A

1 The writer of the newspaper column claims consumers have lost their real food options. Write **two paragraphs**, in which you:

  a identify and explain the examples she gives for thinking this is so

  b explain how the way she expresses herself reveals her own feelings about the subject. You should refer to three or four examples taken from the passage.

Use **your own words** as far as possible and write about **250 words in total**.

2 Explore and comment on the ways in which information, opinions and beliefs are presented in the website material opposite. Explain what you think the writer's purpose is and how successfully you think it has been achieved.

SECTION B

1 Write the words of a talk you would give to students in your Year group in which you inform them of the benefits of a healthy diet and describe some of the foods they should avoid and those they should try to eat more of.

Media text

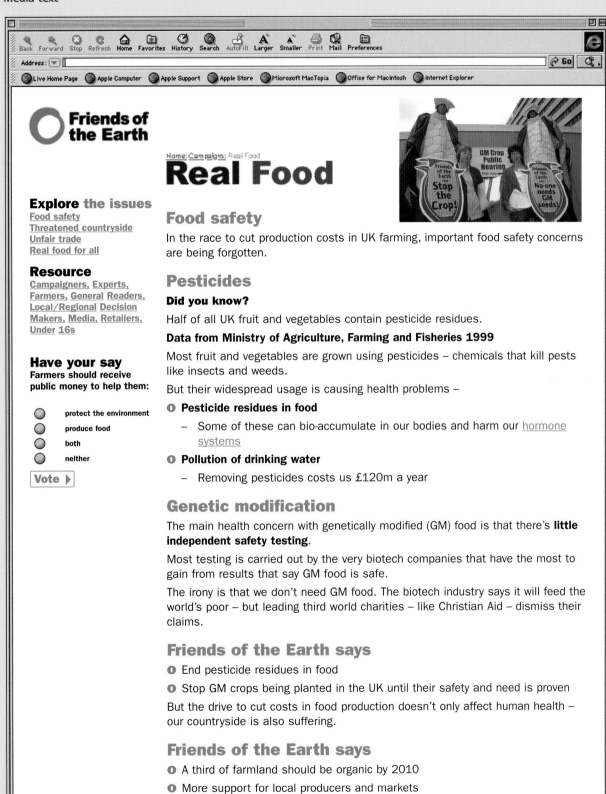

Reviewing your paper

Section A Question 1

The first question is in two parts and asks you to *explain* the writer's view that we have lost our real food options and then to explain how or *analyse* the way this point of view is presented.

What do you need to do?

This question requires you to select and explain specific points. You could plan your answer by listing the points in note form in two columns like this.

Example	Explanation
StarLink Corn	GM crop originally meant as animal feed.
	Mixed with non-GM crops: carried by wind.
	Approved for human consumption.
	Company argued not possible to isolate wind-borne pollen.

Continue the list by adding at least three more examples along with their explanations.

For the second paragraph you are asked to explain *how* the writer reveals her own feelings about the subject. You need to refer to three or four examples. Focus on explaining the effects achieved by the writer's choice of words. For example:

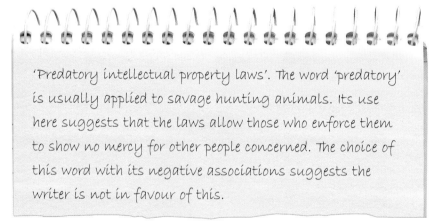

'Predatory intellectual property laws'. The word 'predatory' is usually applied to savage hunting animals. Its use here suggests that the laws allow those who enforce them to show no mercy for other people concerned. The choice of this word with its negative associations suggests the writer is not in favour of this.

Continue with this approach and explain three or four more examples.

 REMEMBER

+ Explain your comments.
+ Refer them back to the wording of the question.
+ Write about the writer's vocabulary and tone.

Section A Question 2

The key words here are *explore*, *comment* and *explain*. This is another *how* question.

Good responses
- ✔ are well organised
- ✔ focus on the question
- ✔ develop the implications of the points they make.

 REMEMBER

The word *explore* suggests that the examiners do not expect any one correct answer. They are looking for how well you can justify the comments you make by reference to the reading material.

What do you need to do?

Structure your response well. Asking yourself the following questions will help you to organise your answer.

- Who has produced this material? Why?
- Who is the target audience?
- What presentation devices are used to attract the readers' attention? (Think about bold print, photographs, etc.)
- Is the material fact, opinion, opinion presented as fact or a mixture of all three?
- How do I know?
- What can I say about the vocabulary and tone of the passage?
- How successful is it? Am I convinced by what it says? How and why has it convinced me (or not)?

Now all you have to do is restate your points in a clearly focused conclusion. Remember, this will be the last thing the examiner will read.

Section B

The writing task asks you to *inform* and *explain*. It gives you a specific audience, purpose and format – the words of a talk.

Good responses
- ✔ use an oral register effectively
- ✔ make some attempt to use rhetorical devices.

 REMEMBER

This is an English not a Biology examination. Examiners will not expect your arguments to be too technical. They will, however, expect them to be well structured and with sensible justifications for your comments.

Different cultures, analysis and argument

In this part of your course, and in the examination that you take, you will develop and demonstrate your **reading** skills (Section A) and **writing** skills (Section B).

Section A requires you to produce *one* written response based on your reading and study of a literary text written by someone from a different culture.

This is worth 10% of the total marks for English.

Section B requires you to produce *two* different pieces of writing – one that is designed to **review**, **comment** or **analyse**, and another designed to **advise**, **argue** or **persuade**.

Each of these is worth 10% of the total marks for English.

 The particular skills (**Assessment objectives**) involved in this Unit are listed below.

In **Section A**, you will need to:

> ✔ read the texts closely
> ✔ develop your own understanding of and response to the texts
> ✔ explore the ways in which writers use language and structure their texts
> ✔ explain how writers convey characters, settings, themes and culture
> ✔ write about a text by referring to it in detail.

The same texts may be studied and similar passages set at both Foundation and Higher Tier. However, the tasks set and the quality of work expected are different.

In **Section B** you will need to:

> ✔ write clearly and imaginatively
> ✔ use language suitable for different readers and purposes
> ✔ organise your writing into sentences, paragraphs and whole texts
> ✔ use different kinds of sentences
> ✔ spell and punctuate your work accurately.

Reading literature from different cultures

SECTION A

In this section, you will study examples of stories written by authors from different cultures. We will examine extracts from the texts to help you develop the understanding and skills you need for this part of the examination.

The Examination Board suggests several alternative texts for use in this Unit; however, most of the extracts used here are drawn from *Opening Worlds*, the OCR Anthology.

You are also recommended to consult the companion title, *Working with Opening Worlds and Opening Lines*.

Different cultures

The texts you will study in this part of your GCSE English course are all written by people whose **culture** is probably different from your own. Reading stories like this can teach us much about the lives and experiences of other people, as well as amuse, entertain and move us.

In this section we will start to look closely at two important aspects of these texts:

- what the texts reveal to us about different lives and cultures
- how writers create different effects and convey impressions of their cultures in their stories.

First, though, we need to be clear about what we mean by the word 'culture'.

ACTIVITY 1

Listed in the table below are a number of possible factors that help make us the way we are, and make up our particular way of life.

Copy the table. Working in groups, place the factors in a rank order of importance, saying which of them is the *most* important (1) and which is the *least* important (6) in defining your culture or way of life. Use the Comment column to make a note of the main points from your discussion.

Factor	Rank order	Comment
The language you speak		
The clothes you wear		
Your religion		
The food you eat		
The climate and environment		
The kinds of work you do		
How you spend your spare time		
The things you believe to be important and valuable		
The traditions, holidays and festivals you celebrate		

Whatever order you decided to put these factors in, all of them are likely to play some part in making up a particular culture. As you read the texts you are studying for this part of the exam, keep a record of the ways in which each writer reveals these various aspects of their culture.

ACTIVITY 2

If you are using the OCR Anthology, *Opening Worlds*, you might find it useful to record some examples of these various aspects of different cultures. To help you do this, complete the following questions as you read the stories in the collection.

1 **Language:** In *The Red Ball*, how does the language of the boy's father differ from standard English?

2 **Religion:** In *Dead Men's Path*, how do the ancient, traditional religious beliefs differ from those of the headteacher?

3 **Climate and environment:** What do you learn about the climate and environment of Thailand as revealed in *The Gold-Legged Frog*?

4 **Beliefs and values:** *The Tall Woman and Her Short Husband* describes what happens when there is a revolutionary change in beliefs and values within a society. What is this change, and how does it affect people in the story?

5 **Traditions and festivals:** How are the traditions associated with marriage and weddings in *Snapshots of a Wedding* different from those in your culture?

Look also for examples of the same aspects of culture in the other stories you read, as well as in the stories specified.

Getting a story started: opening paragraphs

As you begin to read the stories in *Opening Worlds* (or other narrative texts) you will meet many different methods of starting a story. Some of the most common are:

- giving a description of the setting or situation
- going straight into some dialogue between two or more of the characters
- offering a description of one or more of the characters
- going straight into part of the action or narrative.

 ACTIVITY 3

Work in groups. Read the three texts below and on page 66, each of which is the opening of a story in *Opening Worlds*.

1 First decide which of the starting methods listed above each writer is using.

2 Then consider the advantages and disadvantages of each starting method.

Record your ideas in a table like the one below.

Text	Method(s)	Advantages/Disadvantages
1		
2		
3		

Text 1

Wedding days always started at the haunting, magical hour of early dawn when there was only a pale crack of light on the horizon. For those who were awake, it took the earth hours to adjust to daylight. The cool and damp of the night slowly arose in shimmering waves like water and even the forms of the people who bestirred themselves at this unearthly hour were distorted in the haze; they appeared to be dancers in slow motion, with fluid, watery forms. In the dim light, four men, the relatives of the bridegroom, Kegoletile, slowly herded an ox before them towards the yard of MmaKhudu, where the bride, Neo, lived. People were already astir in MmaKhudu's yard, yet for a while they all came and peered closely at the distorted fluid forms that approached, to ascertain if it were indeed the relatives of the bridegroom. Then the ox, who was a rather stupid fellow and unaware of his sudden and impending end as meat for the wedding feast, bellowed casually his early morning yawn. At this, the beautiful ululating of the women rose and swelled over the air like water bubbling rapidly and melodiously over the stones of a clear, sparkling stream.

From *Snapshots of a Wedding* by Bessie Head

Text 2

The piercing bell that announced the beginning of the school day had hardly died down when Anna Vasilevna came into the class-room. The children stood up in a friendly way to greet her, and then settled down in their places. Quiet was not immediately established. There was a banging of desk lids and a squeaking of benches, and someone sighed noisily, apparently bidding farewell to the serenity of the morning atmosphere.

(*The Winter Oak* by Yuri Nagibin)

Text 3

'Aye ... Thinny Boney! You want to play?'
    One of the boys called out to him, and although he had heard and knew they were calling him, he kept pulling out the red petals of the hibiscus flower ...
    'Match-stick foot! You playin' deaf. You want to play or you don't want to play?'

From *The Red Ball* by Ismith Khan

Beginning, middle and end: the structure of stories

What makes a story? Many people would suggest that a story needs a 'beginning, middle and end', so that we feel some satisfaction and enjoyment when we have finished reading it.

One simple way of looking at this is to analyse a story in terms of stages. We can use a simple children's story such as *Goldilocks and the Three Bears* as an example.

Stage	What happens	Example
1 Opening	The important details about a situation are established – characters introduced, setting or situation described.	Goldilocks goes for a walk in the woods; meanwhile, three bears get ready for breakfast and leave their cottage.
2 Development	Something happens to change, complicate or cause a problem in this situation.	Goldilocks goes into the cottage and starts to try the chairs, the porridge and the beds.
3 Crisis	The climax of the story – the problem or complication comes to a crunch.	The bears return to find evidence of Goldilocks' intrusion!
4 Resolution	The 'ending' – either good or bad.	Goldilocks runs away!

ACTIVITY 4

For any of the stories in *Opening Worlds*, or other stories that you are studying, decide which parts of the story correspond to the different stages you looked at for *Goldilocks and the Three Bears*.

Does this structure work for *all* the stories?

When we write a story, we can choose to arrange the events of the story in different ways. The most obvious way is to start at the beginning and go right through to the end, but sometimes different effects can be achieved by starting the narrative towards the end of the story, and using a **flashback** to what has happened previously. You can probably think of films that do this.

For example, when we start to read *The Gold-Legged Frog*, it is already near evening – but the main events of the story have actually taken place earlier that day. So Mr Nak Na-ngam's early morning walk with his son, the cobra bite that the son suffers, the son's illness, the desperate attempts to cure the effects of the snake bite, and Mr Nak Na-ngam's humiliating visit to the government office are all told to us via a flashback that begins: 'As he recalled the biting cold of the morning, he thought again of his little son.'

ACTIVITY 5

Read the whole story of *The Gold-Legged Frog*. Note the place, fairly near the start of the 'flashback' section, where we read 'If only he had gone home then, the poor child would be all right now.'

1 What questions does this sentence put in your mind as you read the story?

2 What possible effects of the 'flashback' method do you think it illustrates?

Points of view

When we tell a story, we can choose to tell it from several different viewpoints. Sometimes, the storyteller – the **narrator** – is a character who is also part of the story itself, as in Amy Tan's *Two Kinds*, which starts:

> My mother believed you could be anything you wanted to be in America. You could open a restaurant. You could work for the government and get good retirement. You could buy a house with almost no money down. You could become rich. You could become instantly famous.

When the storyteller refers to him/herself as 'I' or 'me' the writer is choosing to tell the story in the **first person**.

Alternatively, the storyteller may be someone who is not actually part of the story, but an outsider looking in. This kind of story will talk more about 'her' and 'him' and is being told in the **third person** as in the opening of R. K. Narayan's *Leela's Friend*:

> Sidda was hanging about the gate at a moment when Mr Sivasanker was standing in the front veranda of his house, brooding over the servant problem.

There are different possibilities – and limitations – which a writer faces using these different viewpoints for the narrator.

ACTIVITY 6

From the list of effects listed below, decide whether each one is easier to achieve using a **first** or **third** person narrator.

Effects	First person	Third person
Reveals a lot about the thoughts and feelings of the main character		
Makes you sympathise with the central character		
Gives a clear unbiased view of things		
Only one point of view is really presented		
Difficult to convey what a character is really thinking		
Can use the character's own language to tell the story		

Sometimes a third person narrator can try to 'get inside the head' of one of the characters by adopting the same kind of language that the character might think in.

ACTIVITY 7

Read the following extract from *Games at Twilight*. Working in groups, suggest how the writer has tried to capture the thoughts and feelings of the boy, Ravi, who has successfully hidden from Raghu during a game of hide-and-seek.

Ravi sat back on the harsh edge of the tub, deciding to hold out a bit longer. What fun if they were all found and caught – he alone left unconquered! He had never known that sensation. Nothing more wonderful had ever happened to him than being taken out by an uncle and bought a whole slab of chocolate all to himself, or being flung into the soda-man's pony cart and driven up to the gate by the friendly driver with the red beard and pointed ears. To defeat Raghu – that hirsute, hoarse-voiced football champion – and to be the winner in a circle of older, bigger, luckier children – that would be thrilling beyond imagination.

From *Games at Twilight* by Anita Desai

Creating a character

How can a writer bring a character to life in just a few lines?
There are three things s/he can do:

- give some vivid physical description
- describe the distinctive things a character does
- use dialogue to convey the way a character speaks.

ACTIVITY 8

Look at the extract on page 70 from *The Tall Woman and Her Short Husband*, which describes the two central characters.

1 First, say which of the three methods for creating a character the writer uses here.
2 Then try to put into your own words the impressions you receive of these characters.
3 Now note down the particular words or phrases that convey these impressions vividly.

She seemed dried up and scrawny with a face like an unvarnished ping-pong bat. Her features would pass, but they were small and insignificant as if carved in shallow relief. She was flat-chested, had a ramrod back and buttocks as scraggy as a scrubbing board. Her husband on the other hand seemed a rubber rolypoly: well-fleshed, solid and radiant. Everything about him – his calves, insteps, lips, nose and fingers – were like pudgy little meatballs. He had soft skin and a fine complexion shining with excess fat and ruddy because of all the red blood in his veins. His eyes were like two high-voltage little light bulbs, while his wife's were like glazed marbles.

From *The Tall Woman and Her Short Husband* by Feng Ji-cai

Now let's consider how dialogue, or **direct speech**, can convey character. In the following extract from *The Red Ball*, the central character of the story, whose family has recently moved to Port of Spain, returns home late to be confronted by his father.

'Boy, where you does go whole evening instead of stop home here and help your moomah?' his father asked ...

'Nowhere,' he answered ...

'No-way, no-way ... You beginning to play big shot! You could talk better than you moomah and poopah. Boy! You don't know how lucky you is to be goin' to school. When I was your age ...' His father left the sentence incomplete as he put the nip [of rum] to his mouth and gargled the rum as though he were rinsing out his mouth, then swallowed it.

'Leave the child alone! If that is the way they teach him to talk in school, that is the right way,' his mother put in his defence.

From *The Red Ball* by Ismith Khan

The variety of English spoken by the father here is sometimes called **Creole** English. Some of its vocabulary, grammar and pronunciation are unlike what we know as standard English, partly as a result of the influence of African languages once spoken by slaves when they were first brought to the Caribbean and North America.

ACTIVITY 9

Read the extract above carefully. Then work in groups to discuss the following.

1 Identify some of the ways in which the father's speech is different from standard English.

2 Why do you think the boy's pronunciation is different from his father's?

3 What does the extract show us about the parents' characters and attitudes?

Creating a setting

Writers often use descriptions to convey a strong impression of the settings in which their stories take place. In the examination, you need to be able to explain some of the ways in which they do this.

ACTIVITY 10

Work in groups. Look again at the opening of *Snapshots of a Wedding* by Bessie Head (see page 65) and consider the table below.

1 Try to agree on which words or phrases in the first column of the table you would use to describe your impressions of the atmosphere the writer is trying to create here.

2 Then look at the groups of words and phrases in the second column, taken from the extract. In the third column assess what the words or phrases within each group have in common, and how they help create any of the impressions you have suggested.

Impressions	Words and phrases	Assessment
◆ Mysterious ◆ A slow dawn ◆ Refreshing ◆ Exciting ◆ Mystical ◆ An air of anticipation ◆ Sluggish ◆ Tranquil ◆ Beautiful ◆ Dull	Group (a) 'cool and damp' 'shimmering waves like water' 'fluid, watery forms'	
	Group (b) 'people ... bestirred themselves' 'were already astir'	
	Group (c) 'in slow motion' 'slowly herded an ox' 'bellowed casually' 'People ... peered closely'	
	Group (d) 'distorted in the haze' 'distorted fluid forms'	

You may have noticed that good description doesn't just use lots of **adjectives** (such as cool, damp, watery) but may just as easily be conveyed by the **verbs** (peered, bestirred, distorted) and **adverbs** (casually) a writer uses.

What's more, a vivid description of a setting can also evoke a particular **mood** or **atmosphere**. See page 75 for definitions of similes and metaphors and page 78 for definitions of adjectives and adverbs.

ACTIVITY 11

Read carefully the two extracts opposite, each of which describes a setting and conveys atmosphere. Write about your impressions of mood and atmosphere from both extracts and, for each point you make, try to explain how the writer's use of words has made this impression. The framework below may help you.

> One impression I get is that .... The writer conveys this by using words/phrases such as .... and as .... These words suggest/imply that ....
>
> One thing that I've noticed is the way the writer uses adjectives. For example, he describes the .... as '..................'. This conveys the idea of ....
>
> The writer also uses some similes/metaphors in the passage. He compares .... to .... This helps convey the idea of ....

Extract 1

The sun blazed as if determined to burn every living thing in the broad fields to a crisp. Now and again the tall, straight, isolated *sabang* and shorea trees let go of some of their dirty yellow leaves. He sat exhausted against a tree trunk, his dark blue shirt wet with sweat. The expanse round him expressed total dryness. He stared at the tufts of dull grass and bits of straw spinning in a column to the sky. The whirlwind sucked brown earth up into the air casting a dark pall over everything. He recalled the old people had told him this was the portent of drought, want, disaster, and death, and he was afraid. He was now anxious to get home; he could already see the tips of the bamboo thickets surrounding the house far ahead like blades of grass. But he hesitated. A moment before reaching the shade of the tree he felt his ears buzz and his eye blur and knew it meant giddiness and sunstroke.

From *The Gold-Legged Frog* by Khamsing Srinawk

Extract 2

They faced the afternoon. It was too hot. Too bright. The white walls of the veranda glared stridently in the sun. The bougainvillea hung about it, purple and magenta, in livid balloons. The garden outside was like a tray made of beaten brass, flattened out on the red gravel and the stony soil in all shades of metal – aluminium, tin, copper and brass. No life stirred at this arid time of day – the birds still drooped, like dead fruit, in the papery tents of the trees; some squirrels lay limp on the wet earth under the garden tap. The outdoor dog lay stretched as if dead on the veranda mat, his paws and ears and tail all reaching out like dying travellers in search of water. He rolled his eyes at the children – two white marbles rolling in the purple sockets, begging for sympathy – and attempted to lift his tail in a wag but could not.

From *Games at Twilight* by Anita Desai

73

Come to your senses!

When writing a description of a place or setting, good writers often try to appeal to more than one of our senses – sight, sound, smell, touch and taste.

For example, in the opening of *Snapshots of a Wedding*, there are descriptions of things we can see ('a pale crack of light'), things that we can feel or touch ('The cool and damp of the night') and things we can hear ('the ox ... bellowed casually', 'the beautiful ululating ... swelled over the air').

ACTIVITY 12

Read the following extract from *The Red Ball* by Ismith Khan. Use a table like the one below to note the different senses that the writer seeks to engage by his descriptions.

Sense	Example(s)
Sight	
Sound	
Touch	
Smell	
Taste	

'How much *you* want?' the vendor asked, as he stood staring at the heap of hot pink ash in the mouth of the brazier, his thumb hooked in his pants' waist. And again he jerked his shoulders up and down in the same indefinite gesture, and when he thought that the vendor was about to offer him a piece of black pudding for nothing, he moved to the back of the clique of boys and disappeared before the fat old woman turned around to look for him again.

It was turning that salmon and orange light of the evening when the sun's rays and the shadows of the trees in Woodford Square were playing tug o' war, both stretched out thin in the evening as they pulled upon each other until that singular moment when no one was looking, and night fell on the ground like a ball of silk cotton descending through the air with its infinite fall until it touched the grass and settled there as if to remain for ever. He turned into their long tunnelled gateway on Frederick Street and walked to the far end of the deep backyard, for theirs was the last barrack-room close to a high wall that separated the yard from the next street.

As he entered the room he smelt cooking, the smoke of the kerosene lamps, fresh cut grass from his father's clothes, and the faint odour of cigarettes and rum that his father's body exuded.

From *The Red Ball* by Ismith Khan

Similes and metaphors

Similes and **metaphors** are important ways of conveying ideas and getting us to see things differently or vividly. We all use these all the time, as the examples below show. Think of your own examples from everyday speech.

Similes (with 'as' or 'like')	Metaphors ('invisible' comparisons)
As white as snow	You're at the crossroads (An important decision to take)
A face like thunder	An even playing field (Make it fair for everyone)
As daft as a brush	Changing the goal posts (Keep changing the rules)
Like two peas in a pod	Over the moon (Happy)

Both similes and metaphors work by suggesting that two things that you would not usually think of at the same time do actually have something in common. Many of the writers of the stories in *Opening Worlds* make imaginative use of them.

 ACTIVITY 13

Listed below are some similes and/or metaphors from the stories in *Opening Worlds*. For each of them:

1 decide whether a simile or a metaphor is being used

2 explain what the two things being compared have in common and why the comparison is interesting.

The first one has been done as an example.

Simile/Metaphor	Explanation
'The train had cast the station like a skin.' (*The Train from Rhodesia* by Nadine Gordimer)	This is a simile. The train is like a snake because they are both long, narrow and twisty. They both belong to the same environment, i.e. Africa. The platforms surround the train when it is in the station but when it has gone it is like leaving the skin behind.
'The round face was burning and as red from the frost as if it had been rubbed with beetroot ...' (From *The Winter Oak* by Yuri Nagibin)	In this simile, the colour of the boy's face is compared to what it would be like if it had been rubbed with beetroot. This is because ...
'... the birds still drooped, like dead fruit ...' (*Games at Twilight* by Anita Desai)	
'She seemed dried up and scrawny with a face like an unvarnished ping-pong bat.' (*The Tall Woman and her Short Husband* by Feng Ji-cai)	

What's it all about? Themes

A writer may have many reasons for telling a particular story and, of course, will aim to amuse, entertain, intrigue and move his or her readers. However, many of the most interesting stories will also raise important issues or relate to wider questions about life in the writer's society and culture.

We usually refer to these issues or questions as the **themes** of a text.

For example, Chinua Achebe's story *Dead Men's Path* tells how an enthusiastic new headteacher, full of modern ideas, arrives at a village school in Nigeria and closes an ancient pathway that crosses the school grounds. The village priest objects because the path links the village with the cemetery and, according to traditional beliefs, is used by the spirits of the dead to depart, by their ancestors to visit, and by children as they come to the village to be born. The headteacher refuses to allow the path to stay open and, after a young woman dies in childbirth two days later, he finds that the grounds of his school have been trashed.

 **ACTIVITY 14**

Work in groups. Discuss which of the following themes you think Chinua Achebe is exploring in *Dead Men's Path*.

- The conflict between modern and traditional cultures and values.
- The problems of vandalism faced by schools.
- The differences between religious and non-religious ideas.
- The difficulty of bringing about change.
- What happens to people who are too sure of themselves.

There are many different themes explored by the stories in *Opening Worlds*, as in any other text you might be studying. As you read the stories, you should think about what the stories have to say about:

- the differences between different cultures
- the effects of poverty on people
- the pains and difficulties of growing up
- relationships between children and their parents
- love and marriage.

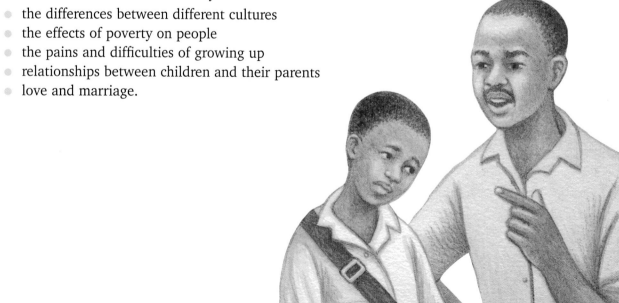

Writing about the texts

When you write about the texts you have been studying you will need to refer closely to them to illustrate your points. There are several ways of doing this.

Refer without quoting

In 'Games at Twilight', the writer uses the third person but still manages to tell the story from the point of view of the central character.

Use a very short quotation in your own sentence

The author of 'The Tall Woman and Her Short Husband' creates a humorous effect by describing the woman as having 'buttocks as scraggy as a scrubbing board'.

Stop to introduce a quotation

In 'Snapshots of a Wedding', the writer starts to build up the atmosphere on the wedding morning right from the start:

'Wedding days always started at the haunting, magical hour of early dawn when there was only a pale crack of light on the horizon.'

To conclude: looking at a whole story

In the last few pages we have looked separately at a number of aspects of story writing. Of course, a good story works because of the way these different parts all combine to produce an overall experience for its readers.

So, when you write about a story in your examination, remember to refer to several of the 'Key Points' on page 78.

KEY POINTS

🔑 **Culture** Which parts of the story reveal things about different aspects of the culture?

🔑 **Character** What impressions do we gain of the main characters? Has the writer used dialogue, descriptions or the characters' actions to convey these impressions?

🔑 **Point of view** From whose point of view is the story told? Is it a first or third person narrative?

🔑 **Language** Does the language reflect the culture or location of the story in any way? Has the writer used similes or metaphors to convey images and impressions?

🔑 **Setting** Pick out some of the details described that help convey to you the setting and atmosphere of the story. Again, comment on the writer's choice of words and any similes or metaphors s/he uses.

🔑 **Structure** Explain how the writer has chosen to organise the main events of the story: how does it begin, what complications or problems arise, and how are these resolved? Point out any use of flashbacks.

🔑 **Themes** Suggest some ideas or issues that the story is 'about'.

Punctuation of speech

When punctuating direct speech take care to use inverted commas around the actual words spoken. There is always a punctuation mark such as a full stop, question mark or exclamation mark *before* the closing inverted commas, *unless* it is followed by 'said' or something similar. In this case, use a comma:
'Well, I don't know,' replied the other.

Adjectives are words used to give information about the things or people they describe, e.g. colours (brown, blue, etc.), textures (rough, smooth) or qualities (unpleasant, exciting).

Adverbs are words used to say how, when or where actions are carried out (e.g. they ran *fast*, he bellowed *casually*).

Standard and non-standard varieties of English

There are many varieties of English spoken in the world. The version that is taught as the 'correct' form of English is known as **standard English**, but many people, even in the United Kingdom, speak with distinctive vocabulary and grammar (**dialect**) or pronunciation (**accent**). Throughout the world, wherever English is spoken, it can have its own local features. The distinctive variety of English spoken in the Caribbean (as in *The Red Ball*), for example, is sometimes called **Creole** English.

Part 1: Writing to review, comment and analyse

In your examination you will be given the task of producing a piece of writing that **reviews**, **comments** and/or **analyses**.

As with any other piece of writing, you will need to take care to write accurately, clearly and in an appropriate style.

However, you also need to practise some of the particular skills associated with writing to review, comment and/or analyse. In this section, we will make clear the difference between these terms, but, as you will discover, there are many similarities and overlap between them. Although the activities you will do focus on each of the three elements separately, in the exam question it is possible that two or more elements will be combined. The specimen paper at the end of this Unit will show how this works in practice.

Reviewing

What do we mean by '**reviewing**' and what is a '**review**'?

ACTIVITY 1

Working in groups, consider the three texts on this page and on page 80. Then copy the table below. Look at the comments in the first column and decide which of them best describes what the writer of the each text is doing (you may wish to tick more than one comment). Make a note of your reasons for choosing and not choosing the comments.

A long time ago, in a galaxy far, far away... someone was fooled into thinking this was a good game!

Star Wars: Obi-Wan

Four films and we have never seen so much as a Pringle jumper.

From the birth of the Rebellion to the death of an Empire, we've never seen Vader teeing off. So why is every baddy from Tatooine to Coruscant trying to brain Obi-Wan with what looks like a golf club?

SWINGING

Like the duff *Power Battles* but in 3D, *Obi-Wan* takes place just before the *Phantom Menace* movie, as we follow the trainee Jedi swinging through 15 levels of gangs on Coruscant, Naboo and Tatooine. Along the way he learns all sorts of new Jedi skills, including throws, telekinesis and even Jedi Bullet Time. Unfortunately, the problem is that young Obi is as flawed as the first

Star Wars movie that he steps from. The levels are barren, boring and repetitive, and the character animation is pretty poor, with 'skating' enemies, shadows that end up in all the wrong places, and thugs who can float in mid-air.

NEGATIVE FORCES

Some of which might be forgivable if the controls weren't so tricky to master. Any old gangster can slaughter a Jedi while they struggle to remember the combination for a Force Push. Worst of all there is slow down – and lots of it. Collect a power-up, receive new orders, or get up-close with the Sand People, and you can create your very own Bullet Time feature – except this one affects everything on screen!

Last on this long list of complaints is the voice of Obi-Wan himself. We didn't exactly expect Ewan McGregor, but this is one Jedi who obviously went to public school. Hoo-rah! Now will someone please explain how a film franchise as brilliant as *Star Wars* produced a game as bad as this?

Softography
These guys have also made...

Star Wars Ep 1: Jedi Power Battles	68%
Star Wars Episode 1: Racer	84%
Escape from Monkey Island	90%
Star Wars: Dark Forces	76%
Jedi Knight 2	N/A
Star Wars: Galactic Battlegrounds	80%

Text 1
Review of Obi-Wan Computer Game from *Games Master* magazine March 2002

Comments	Text 1	Text 2	Text 3
Gives us facts about an event or product but no opinions			
Tells us what is good and bad about something			
Gives us personal opinions but very few facts			
Suggests how something could be improved			
Tells us some information about an event or an experience and suggests what was good and bad about it			
Tells us the complete story of an event/film/programme			

Text 2

Review of Progress: Autumn Term   **English**

This term we have been studying Much Ado About Nothing and developing writing skills in non-fiction and media. Steven has made some pleasing progress since September and has produced two well-written essays on Shakespeare in which he showed sound understanding of the plot and characters of the play. His discussion work has also been good, though sometimes he needs to listen to others as well as making his own contributions. He has usually produced homework on time but at times his assignments have been rather carelessly presented. To improve further, Steven needs to take more care when checking his work to eliminate some basic spelling and punctuation errors, and try to enlarge his vocabulary by reading as much as he can.

Text 3

The Lord of the Rings

Dec 19 2001

BUY THE TICKET

Starring:	Elijah Wood, Ian McKellen, Viggo Mortensen, Sean Astin, Liv Tyler, Sean Bean
Director:	Peter Jackson
Screen Writer:	Peter Jackson, Fran Walsh, Phillipa Boyens
Details:	178 mins Cert 12 (Entertainment)

IN A NUTSHELL

Passed to him by his cousin Bilbo, young Hobbit Frodo Baggins becomes the unlikely and unwilling bearer of The One Ring of Power, an instrument of unparalleled evil. And so Frodo, along with his three Hobbit chums, the wizard Gandalf and a swordsman named Strider, sets out on an epic quest.

FULL REVIEW

Brooking no argument, history should quickly regard Peter Jackson's *The Fellowship of the Ring* as the first instalment of the best fantasy epic in motion picture history. This statement is worthy of investigation for several reasons. *Fellowship* is indeed merely an opening salvo, and even after three hours in the dark you will likely exit the cinema ravenous with anticipation for the further two parts of the trilogy.

Fellowship is also unabashedly rooted in the fantasy genre. Not to be confused with the techno-cool of good science fiction, nor even the cutesy charm of family fare like *Harry Potter*, the territory of Tolkien is clearly marked by goo and goblins and gobbledegook. Persons with an aversion to lines such as, 'To the bridge of Khazad-dûm!' are as well to stay within the Shire-like comforts of home (their loss).

There are electrifying moments – notably the computer-assisted swooping camera through Isengard as it transforms into a factory for evil. Jackson's screenplay (written in collaboration with Fran Walsh and Phillipa Boyens) is bolder than the surprisingly timid *Harry Potter*.

There are problems, though. The three-hour running time is high on incident and low on form. More importantly, the action clearly climaxes in the desperate flight from the Mines of Moria, where the largely seamless SFX is showcased in the best possible light – total darkness – but the narrative demands a different, downbeat ending. Indeed, but for some fine emotional playing from Bean, Mortensen, Astin and Wood, the final fight might feel like a particularly brutal game of paintball in Bluebell Wood. But then, the real battles are yet to come.

ANY GOOD?

Putting formula blockbusters to shame, *Fellowship* is impeccably cast and constructed with both care and passion: this is a labour of love that never feels laboured. Emotional range and character depth ultimately take us beyond genre limitations, and it deserves to play as wide as a certain Mr. Potter.

COLIN KENNEDY
January 2001

Review of *The Lord of the Rings* edited from empireonline.co.uk

Reviewing may mean doing a number of things, but it will usually involve:

- partly describing something that you have seen or done, or something that you have observed or learned
- mainly evaluating something – saying what is good and bad about it
- suggesting ways in which it could be better
- giving reasons for your judgements.

ACTIVITY 2

Collect a number of reviews from newspapers, magazines and the Internet. Try to find examples of reviews of:

✦ TV programmes ✦ Books ✦ CDs ✦ Concerts ✦ Plays ✦ Films

What makes a good film, TV programme or book? Is it just a matter of opinion, or are there some **criteria** (qualities or standards) on which we can all agree?

When we give a personal opinion, we are offering a **subjective** view of the film, programme or book. When we refer to criteria in a less personal way, we aim to be more **objective**.

In either case, we certainly spend plenty of time arguing about the relative merits of our favourite music, art, books and drama, and most newspapers and magazines carry 'Review' sections in which their critics offer us their views of the most recent releases.

 ## ACTIVITY 3

Copy the table below and consider the list of criteria that we might use to try and **evaluate** a film.

1 First, decide individually how important you think each of the criteria is in deciding how good a film is, ranking them from 1 (*most* important) to 10 (*least* important).

2 Then, in groups, compare your rankings and try to agree on a rank order. Your discussion will be most interesting if you can suggest examples of films that you think have these qualities – make a note of these films in your table.

Criteria	Importance (rank from 1 to 10)	Your examples
It has an underlying theme or 'message'; makes a serious point		
It has characters you like and identify with		
It has a good soundtrack		
It has exciting action sequences		
It is true to life and the story is believable		
It has good dialogue		
It has a strong emotional impact		
Unexpected twists in the story		
It includes some humorous dialogue or action		
It makes you think		

81

ACTIVITY 4

Think of a film or video that you have seen recently and prepare a short talk in which you offer a review as part of a radio or TV programme about films.

KEY POINTS

🔑 When planning a short talk you should aim to make brief notes only – these will act as prompts and remind you what to talk about next.

🔑 *Don't* try to write out your talk in full – no one wants to watch and listen to someone just reading out from a sheet of paper.

🔑 It is better to use postcard-size cue cards, one for each section of the talk.

🔑 Remember, reviewing means **evaluating**, not just *repeating* the story.

If you have access to computer and projection facilities, instead of cue cards, you could use PowerPoint to prepare and present your talk.

Make some notes for your talk following the plan set out on the cue cards below.

1
+ What was the film?
+ Who starred in it?
+ Give a few details of the setting and plot.

2
+ How does the story start?
+ How fast-moving is it?
+ Are there any unexpected twists? (N.B. Don't give them away!)
+ Is the ending predictable or surprising?

3
+ Say something about the different characters – are there heroes, villains, humorous characters, etc.?
+ How well did the actors portray the characters?

4
+ Comment on other aspects of the film, e.g. the special effects, music soundtrack, etc.
+ Did the film make you think and have an emotional impact on you?
+ Did the film have a serious point, or was it just escapist entertainment?

As we saw earlier, reviewing needn't apply only to books, films or CDs. It can also describe the way we look back over an activity, event or experience and weigh up strengths and weaknesses in order to improve in future.

 **ACTIVITY 5**

Choose from the following tasks.

1 Write a review of a book/film/CD that you have read/seen/heard recently. Try to follow a plan similar to the one for the short talk above.

2 Think about an event you have experienced recently – perhaps a school trip, concert or performance. Write a review in which you:
   - briefly **describe** the event itself
   - **evaluate** the successful aspects of the event (try to be **objective** as well as **subjective**)
   - point out any problems and suggest improvements for next time.

Many websites now invite people to contribute their own reviews of books, films, CDs, etc. Try submitting one of your reviews to a site such as Amazon.co.uk

Some useful words and phrases for this section

Criteria	Evaluate	Objective	Subjective

Subjective opinions may be introduced with phrases such as:

In my opinion
It seems to me that
I felt that
It struck me that

Objective evaluations may often be expressed:

without referring to 'I' (= the first person)
using less emotional language
giving clear reasons for any views expressed

Positive and negative features may be contrasted by using words/phrases such as:

however
on the other hand
whereas

Suggestions for improvements may often be expressed by using words/phrases such as:

could have
ought to
it might have been better to

Commenting

Commenting is what we do when we respond to something that someone else has said, done or written with a considered view of our own.

Commenting is part of reviewing, but many other kinds of writing that are not reviews also require you to comment. This may involve:

- agreeing or disagreeing with what someone has said or written
- pointing out what is good and bad, or right and wrong, about a situation or an idea
- offering your own opinion about a topic together with some reasons for this.

 ACTIVITY 6

The article below is a 'Comment' column in a monthly football magazine.

When you have read the article, make a written note of:

1 words and phrases that express the writer's agreement with and approval of what others have said or done

2 words or phrases that do the opposite and express the writer's disagreement

3 parts of the article where the writer is clearly offering a personal opinion

4 parts of the article where the writer gives reasons for his views.

COMMENT

WHAT A MONTH for football! Hooligans, red cards, fights, flying pies … let's hope this is not a return to the bad old days. I don't believe it is.

There have been a number of unsavoury incidents which we could do without. And I think the authorities or the clubs concerned should act fast to nip these problems in the bud.

Full marks to Leeds boss David O'Leary for saying the club will clear out any players who don't toe the line. Let's hope they stick to that promise.

Full marks to Spurs for saying they will ban for life any 'fan' throwing objects at White Hart Lane. Let's hope other clubs take similar action.

Full marks to Sam Hammam, the Cardiff chairman, for deciding not to do his pitch side walk anymore. I know he has now been told officially that he can't, but he acted first.

Now back to that prickly subject of discipline. We have seen a number of games this season where the yellow – and sometimes red – cards have been brandished with some abandon by referees.

What has annoyed me, probably like many other fans and certainly players and managers, is that there has been no consistency. One player appears to be able to get away with a tackle whilst one very similar is judged as a foul in the same game.

I'm all for the game being correctly ruled by the officials, so long as everyone is treated in the same way. Let's see some sense over hard tackles – it appears football is destined to become a non-contact sport with no determined challenges.

Colin Mitchell

Colin Mitchell, Editor

© Colin Mitchell/Shoot Monthly/IPC Magazine

From Shoot Monthly

ACTIVITY 7

Now look at the following texts on the topic of the smacking of children.

Text 1 (below), from an article in the *Guardian* newspaper, asks 'Should parents be allowed to smack?'. Text 2 (on page 86) is a Letter to the Editor of a local newspaper.

One of the texts sets out mainly to give some **information** about and raise the issue of smacking, and one is clearly **commenting** on the issue.

First say which is the information article and which the comment article, then list some of the differences between the articles.

Text 1

Should parents be allowed to smack?

In a few weeks' time, the Scottish parliament will debate proposals to ban the smacking of children under three, and to outlaw the use of implements to discipline a child of any age. The Scottish decision could well set a precedent for the rest of Britain.

Late last year, the government in Westminster decided not to introduce a law prohibiting the smacking of children in England and Wales. This followed a nationwide consultation, prompted by a 1998 European Court of Human Rights ruling that Britain had failed to protect a nine-year-old boy whose father had hit him with a garden cane. At the time, Jacqui Smith, a health minister, said that 70% of those people consulted felt smacking should not be outlawed.

Children's charities were outraged at the decision – the NSPCC said it was akin to declaring 'open season on hitting babies and toddlers'. Save the Children said: 'Our evidence is that most parents don't like smacking, they just don't know what else to do.'

Smacking has long been deemed an acceptable form of discipline in Britain. Indeed, many British adults were raised in an environment where bad behaviour at school resulted in some form of corporal punishment, such as caning.

In 1994, a government survey into corporal punishment in the home found that 75% of children under one had been smacked and that one quarter of children under seven had been 'severely punished' – meaning punished with the use of implements, punished with a risk of injury, punishment over a prolonged period of time or regular, repeated punishment.

Tony Blair himself has admitted to smacking his children. In a 1996 interview with Parents magazine, he said: 'When my children were little, I smacked them occasionally if they were really naughty, or did something nasty to another child. But I always regretted it because there are lots of ways of disciplining a child and I don't believe that belting is the best one.'

...

During the Scottish parliamentary debate, Save the Children commissioned a survey of some 1,300 children across Scotland to gauge their opinions on smacking. It was the first time that children had been consulted on this matter. The survey reported that 94% of children believed there were other ways of disciplining youngsters, such as withholding pocket money, making them perform chores, or preventing them from seeing their friends. The children stated that all of these would be preferable to smacking.

Three-quarters said it was absolutely wrong for an adult to hit a child. Asked how they felt after they had been smacked, their adjectives included: terrified, disliked, lonely, sick and ashamed. 'Smacking,' said one seven-year-old boy, 'makes you angry and you hate your parents for five hours.' Nine-year-old Amy put it most succinctly: 'A big person should not hit a small person.'

Laura Barton, *Guardian Education*, 5/3/02

Text 2

> Dear Editor,
>
> So the do-gooders are now telling us that we cannot smack our children to teach them what's right and wrong! No wonder we see increasing numbers of young people on the streets and in the courts, committing burglaries and taking drugs. No one wants to see very young children being badly beaten but a firm smack to let them know they have crossed the line never did anyone any harm. Maybe children under 3 shouldn't need to be smacked, but older children need a bit of discipline when they are growing up – just like folks of my generation had – and there are times when a stiff talking to is just not enough. As they used to say, 'spare the rod and spoil the child'.
>
> Besides, for the government to interfere with the way parents bring up their own kids is just barmy. Mums and dads are the best ones to judge when a telling off will do, or if a firm smack is needed to teach their children a lesson.

 **ACTIVITY 8**

Work in groups. Discuss and make your comments on the issues, ideas and views expressed in the articles and the letter.

1 Which parts of each surprise you, shock you or make you think?

2 Which parts do you agree with? Or disagree with?

3 As a group, decide which *one* of the following statements best describes your views on the subject.

- It should be against the law to smack any children.
- It should be against the law to smack children under three years.
- Smacking of children should be allowed.

4 One person should report back from your group to the whole class. **Summarise** the main points of your discussion and **give reasons** why you agreed on the statement you chose.

 **ACTIVITY 9**

Now write your response to the letter (Text 2). You might find it helpful to use the following frame.

1st paragraph	Refer to the letter and say in general whether or not you agree with it. Refer also to Laura Barton's article.
2nd paragraph	What do you think about the distinction in the letter between children under and over three years old?
3rd paragraph	Do you agree that the present generation is as bad as the writer of the letter says? Give reasons.
4th paragraph	Do you think that smacking is the best or only way of disciplining children? Refer to Laura Barton's article here.
5th paragraph	Briefly sum up your position and opinion.

When commenting, try to do the following

Signal agreement: First person singular ('*I agree that*'), first person plural ('*why don't we*') and exclamations ('*what a good idea!*').

Signal disagreement: First person singular ('*I don't agree with*').

Express doubt: Ask questions ('*Why should this be allowed?*').

Repeating: Make strong patterns in your writing by repeating phrases ('*Full marks to … full marks to …*').

Paragraphing: Usually start a new paragraph for a new point or idea. In popular newspapers and magazines, paragraphs are often quite short – maybe one or two sentences. They may be longer in other kinds of writing you do.

Analysing

Analysis is a word that is often used in many different situations and has several meanings.

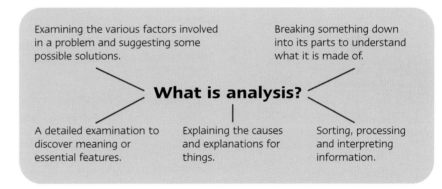

Examining the various factors involved in a problem and suggesting some possible solutions.

Breaking something down into its parts to understand what it is made of.

What is analysis?

A detailed examination to discover meaning or essential features.

Explaining the causes and explanations for things.

Sorting, processing and interpreting information.

 ACTIVITY 10

Some examples of situations where we carry out analysis are listed in the table below. Working in groups, decide for each of these situations what you think the person carrying out the analysis actually *does*, and which of the definitions above applies.

Situation	What analysis involves	Which meaning?
A strange substance has been found at the scene of a crime. It is sent to a chemist for analysis.		
You have been carrying out a survey of people's TV viewing habits. You collect 100 completed questionnaires for analysis.		
You have been given a poem to study and asked to analyse it.		
There has recently been an increase in the number of crimes committed in a particular area. A local councillor has been asked to come up with an analysis of the situation.		
A car has developed a strange knocking sound, along with a smell of burning. A mechanic is asked to find the problem and fix it.		

When we analyse something in writing we may be doing something similar to any of the activities described above. However, we can summarise **analysis** quite simply: when we are describing, or informing, or just relating something that has happened, we are writing about **what** is, or was, the situation; when we analyse, we are suggesting **how** or **why** it has come about.

ACTIVITY 11

The following statements (listed **a–j**) are mixed-up pairs about the situations/events/problems listed in the table below. One of each pair is a **what** statement (**description** or **narrative**), the other is a **how** or **why** statement (**analysis**).

1 Match the statements into their pairs.

2 Decide which is the *what* statement and which is the *how* or *why* statement.

3 Copy the table and place the appropriate letters for each event either in column 1 or in column 2.

a England lost 4–0 in a disappointing game last night.

b The effects of worldwide pollution are now being felt, as the build-up of 'greenhouse gases' is causing global warming.

c The exams are getting easier, teachers are getting better, or students are working harder.

d This poem tells us about the feelings of both the boy being bullied, and the bully responsible.

e The fashion industry and the media seem to say to girls: become as thin as the supermodels in the magazines.

f A combination of careless defending and missed chances produced the worst result for years.

g Many scientists now agree that we are witnessing a gradual change in the world's climate.

h There has been a steady rise in the numbers of students achieving Grade C and above over the last ten years.

i Doctors are worried by the numbers of young girls who are developing eating disorders.

j The poet makes the boy's feeling seem real by using the kind of slang phrases you would expect him to use. This helps us feel sorry for the boy.

Situation/event/problem	What statements: description or narrative	How or why statements: analysis
England's defeat in a football match		
A change in the climate		
The increasing pass rate in GCSE examination results		
The number of girls developing eating disorders		
A poem about bullying		

ACTIVITY 12

Your school council meets regularly to analyse problems referred to it for discussion and solution. The agenda for this week's meeting is reproduced below.

1 Working in groups, read the agenda. For each item:
- decide how or why the situation has come about
- suggest possible solutions to the problems
- record the main points of your discussion in a table like the one on page 90.

2 One of the group should then feedback to the rest of the class with your analysis.

ACTIVITY 13

Choose any *one* of the issues listed in the agenda below, and write a letter to your headteacher outlining your analysis of the problem and your solutions.

Try to include some of the useful words and phrases suggested in the frame and the Literacy panel on page 90.

Newtown High School Council Meeting

Agenda Items for Discussion

1 Recently a number of new vending machines selling sweets and snacks have been installed. The funds generated have helped purchase new software. There has been a significant increase in litter throughout and around the school.

2 The school has an outright ban on mobile phones but students want to bring them to school. The school says they are a nuisance in classrooms and that there have been problems with theft in the past. Some students bringing phones have had them confiscated during the day.

3 There has been a series of thefts of students' property recently. These have often been from bags left unattended by students. There are not enough lockers for one per student. The school says there is nowhere to install more. Besides, there have been problems with keys going missing and lockers being vandalised.

Item	Analysis (how and why)	Possible solutions
1 Litter	The main causes of the problem seem to be … The recent increase may be the result of …	One solution might be … We would also like to see …
2 Mobile phones	There seem to be a number of separate issues here. One is … Another is …	One suggestion is …
3 Thefts	There are a number of factors that have contributed to this problem. One is … Another is …	We think one way forward might be …

Some useful words and phrases for this section

Note spellings: *analysis* (the **noun**, or what it is) and *analyse* (the **verb**, or what you do)

Phrases to suggest causes, methods and solutions:

As a result/consequence of …

This was due to …

When we analyse we often suggest explanations/make judgements that *might* be correct but have not been proved. Here are some useful phrases to convey *possible* analysis/solution:

One cause of this may be …

Another possible explanation is …

Some people believe that X is responsible. Others think …

One solution would be …

Another possible step would be to …

Some more topics for writing practice

ACTIVITY 14

1 You are worried about the relatively poor performance of your favourite local sports team. **Review** their performances to date, offer an **analysis** of what you think is going wrong with the team, and suggest how you would introduce improvements.

2 Suppose that there has recently been a worrying increase in graffiti and vandalism in your town centre. **Comment** on this development and **analyse** the causes of the problem before suggesting a solution.

3 Some people at the moment are worried about the amount of crime in some parts of the country. **Analyse** the reasons why you think people commit crimes, and suggest what could be done to improve the situation.

Part 2: Writing to advise, argue and persuade

In your examination you will be given the task of producing a piece of writing that **advises**, **argues** and/or **persuades**.

As with any other piece of writing, you will need to take care to write accurately, clearly and in an appropriate style.

However, you also need to practise some of the particular skills associated with writing to advise, argue and/or persuade. In this section, we will make clear the difference between these terms, but, as you will discover, there are many similarities and overlap between them. Although the activities in this section focus on each of the three elements separately, in the exam question it is possible that two or more elements will be combined. The specimen paper at the end of this Unit will show how this works in practice.

Advising, arguing and persuading: the similarities

We sometimes use language to do three related things.

1 We **advise** other people on what they should or could do in a particular situation or to solve a problem.
2 We **argue** a point of view or opinion – in other words, develop a reasoned point of view or opinion on an issue.
3 We **persuade** others either to agree with our ideas or to do something in response to our appeal.

 **ACTIVITY 15**

Working in groups, brainstorm as many examples as you can of situations when we use *either* speech *or* writing to advise, to persuade or to argue. Here are a few suggestions to get you started.

- Advertisements in magazines and on the TV.
- A careers talk from your teacher.
- A debate or discussion on a controversial topic.
- A letter to the local newspaper.
- An appeal by a charity.
- A leaflet you pick up at the doctor's about smoking.

Record your ideas on a table like the one below, and tick the boxes to show the **purpose** of each example. If you feel you need to tick more than one box for a particular example because it seems to have more than one purpose, then do so.

Situation	Advise	Persuade	Argue

Advising

 ACTIVITY 16

You are going to look at an example of an advisory leaflet designed to give advice to people about how to shop safely on the Internet.

1 First jot down the main things that you think people who are considering shopping on the Internet might be worried about. Use a table like the one below.

2 Then make notes in your table on any suitable advice that you would give people to meet these concerns.

Possible concerns	Advice

3 Now read the leaflet below, which was issued by the government to advise people on safe shopping on the Internet, and answer the following questions.

- How has the writer of the leaflet made it easy to follow?
- What sort of people do you think the leaflet was written for? How can you tell?
- What kinds of vocabulary have been used? Simple/complex? Straightforward/technical? Formal/informal?
- What kinds of sentences have been used? Statements/questions? Commands/instructions? Long/simple/complex?

Safe Internet Shopping

Internet shopping is easy and convenient – by computer, digital TV or mobile phone. This information is to help you buy with confidence.

SAFE PAYMENT
- Your usual consumer rights apply online. In the EU, the card company must refund you if your credit or debit card is used fraudulently.
- If you buy by credit cards and the goods fail to arrive or are faulty, the card company should refund you for any single item costing over £100.

TECHNOLOGY HELPS
- Be aware of the security features on the supplier's website.
- Look for a closed padlock sign at the bottom of the screen, which should appear when you are asked to enter personal details; it shows that your details are protected when being sent.

ONLINE PROTECTION
When you shop on the Internet:
- You must be given key details before you buy (including the supplier's postal address).
- In many cases in the EU the law allows you time to change your mind and get a refund within seven working days of the delivery.
- Items must be delivered within 30 days unless otherwise agreed.

CHECK FIRST
- Use sites you know or which have been recommended to you - or look for the TrustUK logo.
- Check finance offers with the Financial Services Authority.

BUYING FROM ABROAD
- Check technical standards, delivery charges and taxes.
- If you buy from traders in EU countries you have many of the rights you have in the UK.
- Many other countries, such as the USA, have high standards of consumer protection, but check the small print. Your rights are likely to be set by foreign law and problems could be harder to sort out.

DUTIES AND TAXES
- EU: VAT is dealt with by the supplier; no customs duties on goods or services; alcohol and tobacco attract UK excise duty and UK VAT.
- USA and the rest of the world: goods may be liable to customs and excise duties and VAT; rates vary; things delivered digitally online like music are VAT free.

DATA PROTECTION AND UNWANTED E-MAIL
- You have the right to object to the use of your personal details for direct marketing.
- Contact your internet service provider or use the Direct Marketing Association's e-mail preference service.

YOUR HIGH STREET RIGHTS APPLY
- Goods must be of satisfactory quality.
- Adverts and descriptions must not be misleading.
- With auctions and private sellers the general rule is 'buyer beware'.

IF PROBLEMS ARISE
- First, ask the supplier to put things right.
- Many suppliers are covered by schemes aimed at settling disputes without having to go to court. Your local Citizens Advice Bureau can advise further.

FURTHER INFORMATION
Consumer Gateway: www.consumer.gov.uk

Texts 1 and 2 below and on page 94 are advisory leaflets. Text 1 about 'How to make a complaint' is written for young people who are in care or receiving social services. Text 2 about the MMR vaccine is written for parents who are trying to decide how best to protect their babies from the diseases measles, mumps and German measles (rubella).

ACTIVITY 17

Read Text 1 and Text 2 carefully.

1 List some of the similarities in the way the leaflets are organised and present advice.
2 List some of the differences between them that reflect the fact that they are written for different audiences.
3 Rewrite the first part of Text 2 in a style suitable for a rather younger audience.

Text 1

Social Services: Complaints procedure for young people

A COMPLAINT IS WHEN ...
- There are things going on you are unhappy with
- You are being treated unfairly
- There are things you want to sort out

YOU CAN MAKE A COMPLAINT WHEN ...
- You are living at your own home
- You are living with foster carers
- You are living in a residential home
- You are living or have recently left the care of the Local Authority

Step ONE – Talk it over first
Can you talk to someone you trust? ...
- a social worker?
- foster carer?
- someone who works in your residential home?
- Children's Rights Officer?

Usually someone will be able to help ... BUT

- if there's no one you feel you can talk about it with?
- if no one's listening?
- if it hasn't helped?

... then you will need to contact the Complaints and Compliments Unit

Step TWO – How to make your complaint
You can do this in three ways ...
1 Fill in the form at the back of the leaflet and post it off. (No stamp is needed.) You can get someone to help you if you want.
2 Phone the complaints office. The number is on the leaflet. You can explain your complaint over the phone.
3 Or you can ask the complaints officer to come and visit you. The complaints officer's contact details are on the back of the leaflet.

Step THREE – What happens now?
First of all the complaints officer will let you know that your complaint has arrived safely.

Then someone from Social Services will look into the complaint. It might be that they will be able to sort it out after they have talked to you.

It may be better to investigate your complaint formally. Someone from Social Services who has not been involved before will do this. This person is called an 'Investigating Officer'. They will work with an 'Independent Person' to make sure everyone is treated fairly.

Step FOUR
If you are still unhappy and you feel the problem hasn't been sorted out there will be a Review Panel.

This is where a group of people meet to talk about your complaint. The Independent Person will be there. You will be able to go and you can take a friend along with you. The Panel will decide the best thing to do about your complaint.

If you would like some advice ...
because your are unsure whether to complain or just want to talk to someone then contact Children's Rights Calderdale at the address or phone number on the back of the leaflet. They will give you advice about anything that is worrying you.

Text 2

The decision to immunise your child is never simple and you want the facts to help you make that decision. This leaflet provides you with the facts. If you need more information, please talk to your GP, health visitor or practice nurse or contact NHS Direct on 0845 46 47, or visit www.immunisation.org.uk

What is MMR?

MMR vaccine protects your child against measles, mumps and rubella (German measles). It is given to children at 13 months and again before they start school. The second dose protects anybody who did not respond to the first dose. Since 1988 when MMR was introduced in the UK the number of children catching these diseases has fallen to an all-time low.

- Measles can be a serious illness that the vaccine prevents. There are often complications from measles and it can still kill.
- Mumps vaccine prevents mumps, which was the biggest cause of viral meningitis in children.
- Rubella vaccine prevents babies being badly damaged if their mother catches rubella when pregnant.

MMR can prevent these diseases in a combined injection.

What are the side effects of MMR?

MMR contains three separate vaccines in one injection. The vaccines have different side effects at different times.

- About a week to 10 days after the MMR some children become feverish and they may develop a measles-like rash and go off their food. This is because the measles part of the vaccine is starting to work.
- About three to four weeks after the injection a child might occasionally get a mild form of mumps as the mumps part of MMR kicks in.
- In the six weeks after MMR your child may, very rarely, get a rash of small bruise-like spots which may be caused by the measles or rubella parts of the immunisation. This usually gets better on its own. However, if you see spots like this, show them to your doctor.
- Very rarely, children can have severe allergic reactions straight after any immunisation (about 1 in 100,000 immunisations for MMR). If the child is treated quickly, he or she will recover fully. People giving immunisations are trained to deal with allergic reactions.

The risk of serious side effects from the actual disease far outweighs the risk of your child suffering any of the side effects from immunisation.

The table below compares the serious effects of the disease and reactions to MMR.

Condition	Children affected after the natural disease	Children affected after the first does of MMR
Convulsions	1 in 200	1 in 1000
Meningitis or encephalitis	1 in 200 to 1 in 5000	Less than 1 in a million
Conditions affecting blood clotting	1 in 3000 (rubella) 1 in 6000 (measles)	1 in 22,300
SSPE (a delayed complication of measles that causes brain damage and death)	1 in 8000 (children under 2)	0
Deaths	1 in 2500 to 1 in 5000 (depending on age)	0

What about reports of links between autism and MMR? Is this really a risk?

No, autism was well known long before MMR was ever used in this country. Autism, a disorder causing behavioural and language problems, is recognised more often now than in the past and the increases in the cases of autism were going on before MMR was introduced. There was no sudden increase in autism when MMR was introduced. Parents often first notice the signs of autism around the time MMR is usually given. This does not mean that one causes the other.

Extensive research into this possibility shows that there is no link between MMR and autism. These research studies have been carried out in this country, the USA, Sweden and Finland, and involve thousands of children. Experts from around the world, including the World Health Organization, have agreed that there is no link between MMR and autism.

What about reports of links between MMR and bowel disease?

It has been suggested that measles viruses, either from the natural disease or the vaccine, might stay in the bowel and cause bowel disease. But bowel disease is no more common in immunised people than in people who have not been immunised. Again, there have been many studies that cannot find a link with the vaccine. Experts from around the world, including the World Health Organization, also came to the conclusion that the evidence is firmly against any link between measles and MMR vaccines and bowel disease.

Have children been followed up long enough after MMR to know it's safe?

In the USA, MMR has been given for nearly 30 years. Worldwide over 500 million doses have been used in over 90 countries and the vaccine has an excellent safety profile. In Finland where children have been given up to two doses of MMR since 1982, reactions reported after MMR were followed up. Researchers found no deaths, or permanent damage linked to the vaccine. The World Health Organization describes MMR as a 'highly effective vaccine which has such an outstanding safety record'.

Why not give parents choice and let them have single vaccines?

Some people feel that single vaccines might somehow be safer than MMR. But using single vaccines would mean that:

- six separate injections have to be given over a long period of time
- there would be a fall in vaccine coverage as experience shows more children would not complete the course of injections
- children who complete the course are left without protection in the gaps between injections
- babies may catch the disease from their older brothers and sisters who are unprotected between the separate injections
- children who cannot have the MMR vaccine, such as those having treatment for cancer, would be more exposed to infection and
- pregnant women will be at greater risk of rubella infection from their own unprotected children and the children of their friends.

The evidence shows that MMR is a safe and effective vaccine that is not linked to autism. More than 90 countries in the world use MMR and hundreds of millions of children have been protected by this vaccine for nearly 30 years.

It has been said that giving the three vaccines together overloads children's immune systems. This is not the case. Children's immune systems make excellent responses, naturally protecting them against these diseases. No country in the world recommends MMR be given as three separate vaccines. The World Health Organization advises against using separate vaccines because they would leave children at risk for no benefit.

MMR - the facts

MMR vaccine protects children against measles, mumps and rubella.

- In nearly 30 years, over 500 million doses of MMR have been given in over 90 countries. It has an excellent safety record.
- The evidence is against any link between MMR and autism or bowel disease.
- The practice of giving the vaccines separately may be harmful. It leaves children open to the risk of catching measles, mumps or rubella.
- Where MMR is available, no country recommends giving the vaccines separately.
- Measles is a highly infectious disease and it kills and disables children and adults.
- In the year before MMR was introduced in England, 86,000 children caught measles and 16 died. A recent outbreak in Dublin, caused by parents not having their children vaccinated, left three children dead.
- Mumps was the leading cause of viral meningitis in children before the MMR vaccine was introduced. Now it is virtually eliminated.
- The damage rubella can do to unborn babies is devastating - in many cases pregnant women catch rubella from their own or their friends' children.
- MMR protects your child and your family against measles, mumps and rubella. Because of MMR these three diseases are no longer risks. If children go unprotected, the diseases will come back.

If you missed your MMR appointment, you can get the immunisation at any time.

ACTIVITY 18

Now try to put into practice some of the methods of advisory writing you noted in Activities 16 and 17. Use the panel on 'Features of writing to advise' (page 96) to help you.

1 Giving up smoking

Some points that have been taken from an advice leaflet designed to help people give up smoking are on the note pad below.

Use some of these points to create a piece of advisory writing of your own.
This could be a leaflet aimed at *either* younger readers *or* mature, older readers.

Suggested points on giving up smoking

- Prepare yourself for stopping: plan when and how you stop.
- Decide why you want to stop – health, money, smells, fitness, antisocial.
- Tell friends and family – especially your smoking friends.
- Consider use of patches/chewing gum.
- Change your eating and drinking habits.
- Get rid of lighters, ashtrays, etc.
- Get something to fiddle with.
- Reward yourself each day.
- Take up some physical exercise.
- Keep the money you would have spent – and save it for a holiday or night out.
- Ring the Quitline 0800 002200.

2 Bullying

Consider the following letter, submitted to a 'Problem Page' section of a magazine by a 13-year-old school student. Write a response in the form of a letter in which you try to give appropriate advice to the writer.

Dear Any Problems

I am writing to you because there is no one else I can turn to. There is a group of people in my class at school who are making my life a misery at the moment. It started with just name-calling but now they are threatening me and asking me for money. Even the person who I thought was my best friend doesn't seem to want to know me. I'm scared that if I tell anyone it will just get worse. Every day now I get up with a sick feeling about having to go to school and face them all. A couple of times I have not been to school at all, and just wandered around town for a few hours until it's time to go home, but I know I can't keep doing this. What can I do?

Features of writing to advise

- Use headings, sub-headings and bullet points to separate points clearly.
- Use questions as sub-headings (e.g. 'What is MMR?') that express the reader's queries or concerns.
- Answer one of these questions directly in each section.
- Deal with each point in a single, fairly short sentence.
- Use the words 'you' and 'your' (the second person) to speak directly to the readers.
- Use sentence structures such as: 'If ... then you should ...'.
- Use vocabulary that is simple enough for most of the 'target' audience to understand.

Arguing

In Unit 1, we suggested a definition of what is meant by an argument (see page 24). Remind yourself of that definition.

One of the places where you find arguments is in newspapers – not usually in the actual reports of events but in the section where the editor gives the newspaper's opinions about issues in the news. This section is called the 'editorial'.

In the following example from the *Daily Express*, entitled 'Motorists are being milked', the editor is writing about some of the measures being introduced to try to reduce traffic congestion and speeding.

Motorists are being milked

Motoring is already expensive enough without the Government finding yet more ways to milk drivers. New figures reveal that a million motorists are now caught speeding every year. Despite that, there are plans to increase the number of speed cameras threefold.

The costs of petrol and road tax are already prohibitive. Now there are proposals to charge drivers for entering city centres, to introduce tolls on major routes and even an idea to charge people for travelling by the mile. These are simply back-door ways for the Government to raise yet more revenue while turning motoring into a preserve of the rich.

Otherwise law-abiding drivers who are just over the speed limit are already being fined £60 a time. Dangerous drivers must be pursued at all costs but the Government must stop persecuting ordinary motorists with ever more speed traps. Cameras are needed at known accident blackspots but they should not be on every street corner just to enable the police to catch some unsuspecting motorist and further fill the Government's coffers.

From the *Daily Express* Editorial

ACTIVITY 19

Read the *Daily Express* article carefully and copy the table below.

1 First decide which of the statements in the table best sums up the point of view being argued by the editor in the article.

2 Then note down the reasons that are offered to support this conclusion.

Statements	Best summary?	Supporting reasons
Most drivers never break the law.		
The Government is picking on motorists unfairly and should stop making motoring more and more expensive.		
The Government is right to target speeding motorists.		
There should be more speed cameras to improve road safety.		

3 Now look at how the writer uses language to reinforce his point of view. Comment on the effect of the parts of the following phrases in bold.

- 'Motorists are being **milked**'
- '**Otherwise law-abiding drivers** who are **just** over the speed limit are already being fined'
- 'The Government **must** stop **persecuting ordinary motorists** with **ever more** speed traps'
- 'Catch some **unsuspecting motorist**'

4 It is not usually very effective simply to dismiss the thing you are arguing against as 'just a load of rubbish'. Note that the writer *does* accept that there is *some* justification for *some* of the measures introduced. Pick out the places in the article where he does this.

Most arguments can provoke either agreement or disagreement. If you disagree with an argument you may wish to respond by putting together your own **counter-argument** which explains why the original argument is wrong. This may involve:

- pointing out some factual errors in the argument
- pointing out some logical errors in the reasoning
- challenging some of the basic ideas in the original
- introducing new information or ideas.

 **ACTIVITY 20**

Work in groups.

1 Try to suggest some possible counter-arguments to 'Motorists are being milked' (page 96) and then compare your ideas with the ones suggested below.

2 Use some of these to write a response to the editorial putting the case *for* the measures that the paper is attacking.

You might find it useful to use some of the following words and phrases to link your argument together.

In your editorial you said .... However .... So ....
Despite the fact that .... Not only .... but also ....
Therefore .... As a consequence ....
Otherwise .... As a result ....

'Motorists are being milked': some possible counter-arguments

- Many people are seriously killed or injured each year as a result of people 'just' exceeding the speed limits.
- Speed limits need to be more strictly enforced to prevent accidents and save lives.
- City centres are becoming increasingly gridlocked with too many cars.
- People need some incentive to use public transport instead of their own cars.
- Cars create much harmful pollution and so people should be deterred from using them.
- Making it more expensive to use cars in cities is one way of doing this.

 Some useful words and phrases for this section

Impersonal tone	Present tense	General pronouns	Connectives

You can make your arguments sound objective and convincing by using:

- an impersonal register: *It can be seen that ...*
- the simple present tense: *I believe that this is so*
- general pronouns or generic terms: *you, people*
- logical connectives between sentences and paragraphs:

  on the other hand, nevertheless, however, although, because, so, finally, in conclusion.

Persuading

Arguing does, of course, involve using good, logical reasons to **persuade** people that what you are saying is right. However, you can also write to persuade people in other ways. You may wish to persuade people to:

- believe that what you are saying is right (e.g. your view about animal experiments or abortion)
- buy a particular product or service (e.g. a new chocolate bar or brand of trainers)
- contribute to a charity (e.g. the NSPCC)
- visit a region or attraction (e.g. your own town or region)
- vote for a person or party in an election (e.g. a candidate for your local council).

When persuading, you will usually use language to appeal to your readers in two ways – appeal to their *heads* and to their *hearts*.

The language of persuasion: heads and hearts

Heads: This means using your **arguing** skills (see above) and putting together facts and information in a **logical** way. You are trying to convince your readers of the truth of what you are saying.

Hearts: This means appealing to your readers' **emotions** by using dramatic, emotional or even exaggerated language to provoke a reaction.

The amounts of head- and heart-related language in a piece of persuasive writing will vary according to the situation in which the piece is written.

Advertising

Writers of advertisements are clearly trying to persuade us to take notice of their products and services. They use a variety of methods to do this.

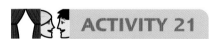 **ACTIVITY 21**

Working in groups, look at the two adverts on page 100. For each one, discuss the ways they try to persuade their readers to consider buying the product. Record your ideas on a table like the one below.

Advert	Head: facts and reasons Which statements or facts tell you positive information?	Heart: feelings Which words convey positive feelings or opinions?
Barnardo's		
Saab		

Help make a real difference to child poverty. Use a Barnardo's Visa credit card.

Fact: One child a week dies following abuse or neglect

You can make a difference

With one in three children living in poverty in Britain today, overcoming child poverty appears to be a daunting challenge. But you could help to make a real difference simply by applying for and using a Barnardo's Visa credit card.

■ Barnardo's will receive £10 as soon as your account is open. That could pay to house a homeless family for one night.

■ Plus Barnardo's will receive a further £2.50 for each subsequent new account after the first 5,000. That's enough to buy hot drinks for a drop in centre for homeless young people.

■ And Barnardo's will receive another 25p for every £100 you spend using the card. That could raise enough in one year to provide school materials for a child with special needs.

Benefits for you too

■ No annual fee, ever. Guaranteed.

■ 5.9% p.a. on balance transfers, fixed until six months after the account is opened. Reverts to a variable rate of 17.9% p.a. 16.5% APR.

■ Discounts off thousands of full brochure priced holidays through the Co-operative Bank Travelclub.

Apply now

Ring today with your bank details to hand for an immediate decision:

0800 0289 289

Lines are open Mon. – Fri. 8am – 9pm, Sat. 8am – 8pm, Sun. 9am – 6pm Please quote ref. 56038 when you phone.

Barnardo's
GIVING CHILDREN BACK THEIR FUTURE
IN PARTNERSHIP WITH

The CO-OPERATIVE BANK

A new form of uplifting

performance

We've taken our award winning Saab 9-5 and revolutionised a few key elements. 1,265 to be exact. These include a turbocharged 2.3 litre engine providing 250bhp. Plus a more responsive chassis, enhanced safety systems and a sleeker aerodynamic design. The result is a premium driving performance, whether you're on the ground or in the air. Call 0845 300 93 95 or visit our website to arrange a 24 hour test drive.

SAAB

Making an appeal

Sometimes you may want to persuade someone to join an organisation or contribute to a charity or campaign. Many advertisements or other types of persuasion work by first painting a black picture of a problem, and then offering a solution. Look at the following example.

COMPASSION IN WORLD FARMING

**BSE
SALMONELLA
E COLI
RIVER POLLUTION
GREENHOUSE GASES
ANIMALS SUFFERING**

What's the connection?

They all emanate from factory farms. In intensive farms the animals are crowded together – pigs on concrete, chickens on excreta-soaked wood shaving. Floors become filthy, disease is rife. The animals' feed may include genetically modified cereals.

It's not surprising therefore that factory farming is bad news for consumers, the environment and, of course, for the animals too, for whom it provides a wretched life. Hens in cages, pigs packed chock-a-block into darkened concrete pens, meat chickens growing so fast they go lame or die from heart disease – it's a dismal scenario.

But there is help at hand. Thanks to Compassion in World Farming's campaigns, some of the cruellest factory farm systems – like battery cages and narrow stalls for calves and pregnant pigs – have been banned or are being phased out at this very moment.

Now Compassion in World Farming (CIWF) needs your support to end the remaining UK factory farming systems and to stop the spread of factory farming world-wide.

Help us bring compassion back to the farm ...

At Compassion in World Farming we believe all farm animals deserve a decent quality of life – access to the outdoors, comfortable lying areas and shelter, good quality food and enough space to mix with other animals in social groups.

Working together

We think you'll agree it doesn't seem too much to ask for. And we know we can achieve these simple goals so much sooner with your help. In the last decade, millions of farm animals have been helped by Compassion in World Farming's campaigns. So do join us today to help the millions still suffering. Please take a moment to fill in the coupon below and help us bring compassion back to the farm.

CIWF

campaigning
for farm animals

ACTIVITY 22

Work in groups.

1 Explain the problem described by the advertisement.

2 Which words or phrases help to convince you how bad the problem is?

3 Identify the solution that the advert offers. How does this convince you that you should contribute to Compassion in World Farming?

ACTIVITY 23

Choose a cause, campaign or charity that you are interested in, and design/write a suitable advertisement intended to persuade people to contribute to it.

Travel and tourism

The town of Barrow-in-Furness in northwest England is not traditionally regarded as a tourist destination. However, the extract below from a tourist leaflet tries to persuade visitors that the town is a pleasant and interesting place to visit.

ACTIVITY 24

Read the tourist leaflet carefully. Working in groups, discuss the ways in which the writer of the pamphlet has tried to persuade you of the town's attractiveness. Make notes about the writer's use of the following:

- layout, presentation and images
- useful information
- adjectives
- lists of things to do and see
- direct speech to the reader
- any other methods.

Welcome to
Barrow-in-Furness

... the historic maritime gateway to the Furness Peninsula. One of the best kept secrets in Britain, Barrow is a Victorian town with a proud heritage of innovation, surrounded by beautiful beaches and inspiring scenery. It is a destination of surprises.

Discover the proud maritime, industrial and social heritage of Barrow-in-Furness at The Dock Museum, Barrow's flagship attraction. A spectacular modern museum straddling an original Victorian Graving Dock. Open all year (closed Mondays except Bank Holidays. Also closed Tuesdays in winter). Tel: 01229 894444. Admission is free.

Furness Abbey, founded 1127, is a magnificent ruin of one of the wealthiest Cistercian abbeys in England (Tel: 01229 823420). The adjacent Custodian's Cottage gives

a fascinating insight into medieval life. Nearby Abbotswood has attractive well marked routes and foot-paths linking the Abbey with Dalton. Piel Castle, a 14th century defensive strong-hold on remote Piel Island, can be reached by ferry. Tel: 01229 835809. Meet the King of Piel in the public house.

Barrow is the Lake District's Premier Shopping Town where major high street names mingle with local specialist shops in a spacious pedestrianised town centre. The big names are in Portland Walk and Dalton Road, whilst surrounding streets tempt you with a wide variety of independent retailers offering exceptional value, variety and personal service. For the bargain hunter, Barrow's Indoor Market has over 100 stalls and is open on Mondays, Wednesdays, Fridays and Saturdays. Barrow has an excellent choice of pubs, cafés, family favourites such as McDonald's, Pizza Hut, KFC, tea shops and restaurants.

Factory shopping bargains can be found on the outskirts of Dalton in Furness at Furness Footwear Factory Shop. Colony Gift Corporation at Lindal in Furness has an excellent factory shop and restaurant. Visitors can try their hand at candle dipping. Tel: 01229 461102.

From Tourism Leaflet, Barrow Borough Council

ACTIVITY 25

Write a short piece about your own town or region. You are aiming to persuade people to visit the area and to make its various attractions sound as interesting as possible.

Making a speech: the art of rhetoric

A public speech can be used to persuade large numbers of people. Some speeches such as Martin Luther King's 'I Have a Dream' speech have become famous as examples of effective, persuasive and inspiring language.

The term **rhetoric** is sometimes used to describe the techniques used to make speaking and writing effective. The speech given by President George W. Bush to the United States Congress following the terrorist attacks on 11 September 2001 illustrates some of these techniques.

We have seen the state of our Union in the endurance of rescuers, working past exhaustion. We have seen the unfurling of flags, the lighting of candles, the giving of blood, the saying of prayers – in English, Hebrew and Arabic. We have seen the decency of a loving and giving people who have made the grief of strangers their own.

My fellow citizens, for the last nine days, the entire world has seen for itself the state of our Union – and it is strong. Tonight we are a country awakened to danger and called to defend freedom. Our grief has turned to anger, and anger to resolution. Whether we bring our enemies to justice, or bring justice to our enemies, justice will be done.

... on behalf of the American people, I thank the world for its outpouring of support. America will never forget the sounds of our National Anthem playing at Buckingham Palace, on the streets of Paris, and at Berlin's Brandenburg Gate. We will not forget South Korean children gathering to pray outside our embassy in Seoul, or the prayers of sympathy offered at a mosque in Cairo. We will not forget moments of silence and days of mourning in Australia and Africa and Latin America.

... Great harm has been done to us. We have suffered great loss. And in our grief and anger we have found our mission and our moment. Freedom and fear are at war. The advance of human freedom – the great achievement of our time, and the great hope of every time – now depends on us. Our nation – this generation – will lift a dark threat of violence from our people and our future. We will rally the world to this cause by our efforts, by our courage. We will not tire, we will not falter, and we will not fail.

... I will not forget this wound to our country or those who inflicted it. I will not yield; I will not rest; I will not relent in waging this struggle for freedom and security for the American people.

From Address to a Joint Session of Congress and the American People, 20/9/2001

Repetition of similar sentences: 'We have seen'

Lists of items: 'the unfurling of flags, the lighting of candles'

Phrases or sentences which contain **pairs of similar ideas**: 'awakened to danger ... called to defend freedom'

Using sets of **contrasts and opposites**: 'Whether we bring our enemies to justice, or bring justice to our enemies'

Use of '**I**' to inspire personal confidence

Use of '**we**' and '**our**' to suggest a sense of unity between the speaker and the audience

A series of three similar items, some of them using **alliteration**: 'We will not tire, we will not falter, and we will not fail'

Using words like '**will not**' that show great determination and confidence

ACTIVITY 26

Imagine that you have to make a speech as part of the elections to your school council.

1 Write the script for the speech you would give. You should seek to persuade people to vote for you by outlining some of your ideas and beliefs that you feel strongly about and convincing your listeners that these are right. Try to make use of some of the persuasive features you read in George Bush's speech.

2 Now have a go at delivering your speech. As you do so, remember to:
   - look up from your script as often as possible
   - vary your tone of voice
   - keep making eye contact with your audience
   - emphasise the main points
   - speak slowly and clearly
   - show some enthusiasm!

Some useful persuasive techniques

- Use facts and statistics to back up your points.
- Use examples of individual people's stories.
- Make sure you organise your ideas logically.
- Use conjunctions such as *so, therefore, however,* to show your reasoning.
- Use adverbs such as *inevitably, undoubtedly, certainly* to emphasise your conclusions.
- Use quotations from well-known authorities on your subject.
- Use some memorable slogans or 'sound-bites'.
- Use alliteration to make some of your phrases memorable.
- Use similes and metaphors to give people strong images.
- Use lists of items, especially lists of three.
- Use repeated sentence structures (parallelism), as in *I have a dream. I have a dream that ... I have a dream that ....*
- Speak directly to your audience using the second person (*you*).

Exam practice

How to approach Section A

You will have already read and studied the texts about which you will write in Section A, so you will be familiar with its content and style. As they are stories from other cultures, you should have given some thought to how aspects of the cultures are revealed.

The examiners will expect you to write a detailed answer, using quotations from and references to the stories to show how well you have understood what happens in them. At Higher Tier especially, you'll need to show how well you've appreciated how the various qualities of the writers' styles succeed in conveying the content effectively to the reader.

 REMEMBER

+ Take your time. Be positive and methodical. Read through all of the question paper before you start to answer the first question.

+ You should spend about 35 minutes on each task. This means you need to allow your brain as much time as possible to think about what you are going to write.

+ Once you know what the writing tasks are you can then start to answer the reading task in Section A. As you do this, another part of your brain will be starting to select ideas for the writing tasks without your being consciously aware of it.

+ Keep yourself clearly focused on the wording of the question. When you're facing the pressures of sitting in an examination room it is very easy to lose sight of the question and start to answer a slightly different one that you may have prepared in advance!

How to approach Section B

When you start to answer the tasks in Section B, do not try to write more than you have time for. The examiners are looking to test your writing skills and your ability to write in two different registers for different audiences. It is your competence in writing accurately and with style that is being assessed. The content of what you write should be relevant, but you will not be expected to demonstrate an exhaustive knowledge of the subject – you won't have time to do so anyway.

 REMEMBER

Section B tests your skills in writing to review/comment/analyse, and advise/argue/persuade. Although we have looked at these areas separately in this Unit, in the exam question it is possible that they will be combined. What is important is that in your writing you use a suitable register for the task.

Practice paper

SECTION A

Read the story *A Gentleman's Agreement* by Elizabeth Jolley, an Australian writer, and then also referring to *one* other story from the *Opening Worlds* anthology, answer the following question (in the real exam *both* stories will be taken from the anthology):

Foundation Tier question

The difficulties and hardships of people's lives cause them to do some unusual things and make some hard decisions. Write about the ways in which such actions and decisions are dealt with in *A Gentleman's Agreement* and *one* other story from the anthology. For each story write about:

a the difficulties in life faced by the characters

b how the writer describes them.

Higher Tier question

Explore the ways in which writers present the hardships and difficulties which some people face in their lives. In your answer refer closely to *A Gentleman's Agreement* and *one* other story from the anthology.

A Gentleman's Agreement

In my home science lesson I had to unpick my darts as Mrs Kay said they were all wrong, and then I scorched the collar of my dress because I had the iron too hot. Then the sewing machine needle broke and there wasn't a spare. Mrs Kay got really wild and Peril Page cut all the notches off her pattern by mistake and that finished everything.

'I'm not ever going back to that school,' I said to Mother in the evening. 'I'm finished with that place!' So that was my brother and me both leaving school before we should have, and my brother kept leaving jobs too, one job after another, sometimes not even staying long enough in one place to wait for his pay.

But Mother was worrying about what to get for my brother's tea.

'What about a bit of lamb's fry and bacon,' I said. She brightened up then and, as she was leaving to go up the terrace for her shopping, she said, 'You come with me tomorrow then and we'll get through the work quicker.' She didn't seem to mind at all that I had left school.

Mother cleaned in a large block of luxury apartments. She had keys to the flats and came and went as she pleased and as her work demanded. It was while she was working there that she had the idea of letting the people from down our street taste the pleasures rich people took for granted. While these people were away to their offices, or on business trips, she let our poor neighbours in. We had wedding receptions and parties in the penthouse and the old folk came in to soak their feet and wash their clothes while Mother was doing the cleaning. As she said, she gave a lot of pleasure to people without doing anybody any harm, though it was often a terrible rush for her. She could never refuse anybody anything and, because of this, always had more work than she could manage and more people to be kind to than her time really allowed.

Sometimes at the weekends I went with Mother to look at Grandpa's valley. It was a long bus ride. We had to get off at the twenty-nine mile peg, cross the Medulla brook and walk up a country road with scrub on either side till we came to some cleared acres of pasture which was the beginning of her father's land. She struggled through the wire fence, hating the mud. She wept out loud because the old man hung on to his land and all his money was buried, as she put it, in the sodden meadows of cape weed and stuck fast in the outcrops of granite higher up where all the top soil had washed away. She couldn't sell the land because Grandpa was still alive in a Home for the Aged, and he wanted to keep the farm though he couldn't do anything with it. Even sheep died there: they either starved or drowned depending on the time of the year. The weatherboard house was falling apart, the tenants were feckless, and if a calf was born there it couldn't get up, that was the kind of place it was.

When we went to see Grandpa, he wanted to know about the farm and Mother tried to think of things to please him. She didn't say the fence posts were crumbling away and that the caster oil plants had taken over the yard so you couldn't get through to the barn.

In the middle of the meadow, there was an old apricot tree; as big as a house and a terrible burden to us to get the fruit at just the right time. Mother liked to take some to the hospital so that Grandpa could keep up his self respect.

In the full heat of the day, I had to pick with an apron tied round me; it had deep pockets for the fruit. I grabbed at the green fruit when I thought Mother wasn't looking, pulling off whole branches so they couldn't be picked later.

'Don't take that branch!' Mother screamed from the ground. 'Them's not ready yet. We'll have to come back tomorrow for them.'

I lost my temper, pulled off the apron full of fruit and hurled it down but it stuck on a branch and hung there quite out of reach.

'Wait! Just you wait until I get hold of you!' Mother pranced round the tree and I didn't come down till we had missed our bus. It was getting dark and all the dogs in the little township barked as if they were insane, as we walked through, trying to get a lift home.

One very cold Sunday in the winter, Mother thought we should go all the same. We passed some sheep huddled in a natural fold of furze and withered grass all frost sparkling in the morning. 'Quick!' Mother said. 'We'll grab a sheep and take a bit of wool back to Grandpa.'

'But they're not our sheep,' I said.

'Never mind!' And she was in among them before I could stop her. The noise was terrible but she managed to grab a bit of wool. 'It's terrible dirty and shabby,' she complained, pulling at the shreds with her cold fingers.

All that evening she was busy with the wool; she did make me laugh. 'How will Modom have her hair done?' She put the wool on the kitchen table and kept walking all round it talking to it. She tried to wash and comb it but it still looked awful so she put it round one of my curlers for the night.

'I don't think I've ever seen such miserable wool. I'm really ashamed of it,' Mother said next morning.

'But it isn't ours,' I said.

'I know, but I'm ashamed all the same,' she said. So when we were in the penthouse at South Heights, she cut a tiny piece off the silky bathroom mat. Later we went to visit Grandpa. He was sitting with his poor paralysed legs under his tartan rug.

'Here's a bit of the wool clip Dad,' Mother said, bending over to kiss him. His whole face lit up.

'That's nice of you to bring it, really nice.' His old fingers stroked the little piece of nylon carpet. 'It's very good, deep and soft,' he smiled at Mother.

'They do wonderful things with sheep these days, Dad,' she said.

'They do indeed,' and all the time he was feeling the bit of carpet.

'Are you pleased, Dad?' Mother asked him anxiously. 'You are pleased, aren't you?'

'Oh yes I am,' he assured her. I thought I saw a moment of disappointment in his eyes, but the eyes of old people often look full of tears.

On the way home I tripped on the steps. 'Ugh! I felt your bones!' Mother was so thin it hurt to fall against her.

'Well, what do you expect me to be, a boneless wonder?' Really Mother had such a hard life and we lived in such a cramped and squalid place. She longed for better things and she needed a good rest. I wished more than anything the old man would agree to sell his land. Because he wouldn't sell, I found myself wishing he would die; it was only that it would sort things out a bit for us.

In the supermarket Mother thought and thought what to get for my brother's tea. All she could come up with was fish fingers and a packet of jelly beans. 'You know I never eat fish and I haven't eaten sweets in years!' My brother looked so tall in the kitchen. He lit a cigarette and slammed out. Mother was too upset to eat her own tea.

Though Grandpa's death was expected, it was a shock to Mother to find she suddenly had eighty-seven acres and the house to sell. She had a terrible lot to do as she decided to sell the property herself and, at the same time, she did not want to let down the people at South Heights. There was a man interested to buy the land; Mother had kept him up her sleeve for years, ever since he had stopped once by the bottom paddock to ask if it was for sale. At the time, Mother would have given her right arm to be able to sell it, but she had promised he should have first refusal if it ever came on the market.

We all three, Mother, myself and my brother, went out at the weekend to tidy things up. We lost my brother, then suddenly saw him running and running and shouting, his voice lifting up in the wind as he raced up the slope of the valley. 'I do believe he's laughing. He's happy!' Mother just stared at him and she looked happy too.

The tenant was standing by the shed. The big tractor had crawled to the doorway like a sick animal and stopped there, but in no time at all my brother had it going. It seemed there was nothing he couldn't do. Suddenly, after doing nothing in his life, he was driving the tractor and making firebreaks; he started to paint the sheds, and told Mother what fence posts and wire to order. All these things had to be done before the sale could go through. We had a wonderful time in the country. I kept wishing we could live in the house; all at once it seemed lovely there at the top of the sunlit meadow. But we all knew that however many acres you have, they aren't any use unless you have money too. No one said anything, though Mother kept looking at my brother and the change in him.

There was no problem about the price of the land; this man, a doctor, really wanted it and Mother needed the money. 'You might as well come too,' Mother said to me on the day of the sale. 'You can learn how business is done.' So we sat in the lawyer's comfortable room as he read out from various papers, and the doctor and Mother signed things. Suddenly she said to them, 'You know my father really loved his farm but he only managed to have it late in life and then was never able to live there because of his illness.' The two men looked at her.

'I'm sure you will understand,' she said to the doctor, 'with your great love of the land, my father's love for his valley. I feel if I could live there just to plant one crop and stay while it matures, he would rest easier in his grave.'

'Well, I don't see why not.' The doctor was really a kind man. The lawyer began to protest; he seemed quite angry.

'It's not in the agreement,' he began to say, but the doctor, silencing him, came round to Mother's side of the table.

'I think you should live there, plant one crop and stay while it matures,' he said. 'It's a gentleman's agreement.'

'That's the best sort,' Mother smiled up at him and they shook hands.

'I wish your crop well,' the doctor said, still shaking her hand. He made the lawyer write out a special clause which they all signed before everyone left satisfied. Mother had never had so much money, the doctor had the valley at last, but it was the gentleman's agreement which was the best part.

So we moved out to the valley; the little weatherboard cottage seemed to come to life very quickly with the pretty things we chose for the rooms. 'It's nice whichever way you look out from these windows,' Mother was just saying, when her crop arrived. The carter set down the boxes along the verandah and, when he had gone, my brother began to unfasten the hessian coverings. Inside were hundreds of seedlings in little plastic containers.

'What are they?' he asked.

'Them,' said Mother, she seemed unconcerned, 'oh they're a jarrah forest.'

'But that will take years and years to mature,' he said.

'I know,' Mother said. 'Tomorrow we'll pick the best places and clear and start planting as we go along.'

'But what about the doctor?' I said. Somehow I could picture him, pale and patient by his car, out on the lonely road which went through his valley. I seemed to see him looking with longing at his paddocks and his meadows and his slopes of scrub and bush.

'Well, he can come on his land, whenever he wants to, and have a look at us,' Mother said. 'There's nothing in the gentleman's agreement to say he can't.'

SECTION B

Foundation and Higher Tier

The material on this page will help you to think about the writing tasks.

SCHOOL UNIFORM

I'm an individual, not a clone. I want to be free to wear what I want so that I can express my personality.

I go to a good school and I'm proud of it. Wearing uniform means that I can show that I identify with what the school stands for.

Students must realise that in some lessons dangly earrings or even very high-heeled shoes can be a danger to health. Anyway, when we have non-uniform days they all wear denim jeans and trainers.

Wearing the school uniform doesn't really bother me. It saves having to worry about what I'm going to put on when I get up in the morning. What really annoys me, however, is when they start to dictate about the length of your hair and the number of earrings you can wear. Why can't I wear a nose stud if I want to?

Writing to review, comment, analyse

1 Give some examples of what you consider to be some of the more unfair school rules (including those concerning uniform) and then give reasons why you and your friends disagree with them.

Writing to advise, argue, persuade

2 A Year 11 student has been suspended from school because s/he has refused to change her/his hairstyle.

Write *two* letters. The first is from the parents of the student to the school's headteacher arguing that their child should be allowed a free choice concerning hairstyle. Then write the headteacher's reply.

Reviewing your paper

Section A

Good responses

- ✔ cover all the points in the question
- ✔ show a clear understanding of the story as a whole
- ✔ make relevant and perceptive comments about the style and structure of the story.

What do you need to do?

1 Read the question carefully. Can you find any clues in the wording to direct the way you respond to it? Some of the points you could make in answer to both Foundation and Higher tier questions might concern:
   - the mother's hard life – no husband – little money – poor housing
   - she works hard – thin and tired
   - she worries that her children are school dropouts
   - the farm provides her son with an aim in life
   - she cares for other people – lets the poor enjoy her employers' apartments.

2 Now find suitable references and quotations to support these points.

3 Think about the writer's choice of words. How do they influence the way you respond to the events and characters in the story?

4 Think about the writer's **tone** and the **attitude** of the narrator. The story is written from the point of view of the mother's daughter and this is somewhat naive. Do you think the writer wants us to endorse fully what the character says and thinks?

❗ REMEMBER

- ✦ A conclusion allows the examiner to review your answer clearly and to assess it fairly.
- ✦ Sum up your main points and relate them back to the question.
- ✦ Explain how far you can defend the mother's actions after considering the evidence.

Section B

Good responses

✔ use correct spelling, punctuation and well-structured paragraphs

✔ show positive merit of vocabulary

✔ use a range of sentence structures

✔ show clear awareness of audience and purpose.

What do you need to do?

✓ Organise your ideas well.

✓ The stimulus material is there to start you off. Try to add ideas of your own.

✓ The two tasks are on similar topics. Brainstorm your ideas first and then decide which points are best suited to which task.

✓ Task 3 requires you to present both sides of an argument. They do not have to be equally balanced. You could match objective reasoning against emotive statements.

 REMEMBER

This is an English examination. Show that you care about the language and take pride in writing it well. Check your writing when you have finished to correct any slips of expression, spelling and punctuation.

And finally ... be polite

You are dealing with a topic about which you may have strong feelings. It's not clever to use the exam to be rude about your own school or headteacher. If you do this you will have used an inappropriate register and the examiner will mark your work accordingly.

Literary heritage and imaginative writing
UNIT 3/4

In this part of your course, you will develop and demonstrate your **writing** and **reading** skills. The assessment of your work may be by examination or coursework.

Unit 3: Examination

Section A requires you to produce *one* piece of writing designed to **explore**, **imagine** or **entertain**.

This is worth 10% of the total marks for English.

Section B requires you to produce *two* pieces of writing, one each based on your study of:

- a play by Shakespeare
- a collection of poetry.

This is worth 10% of the total marks for English (5% each task).

Note: the work you submit on Shakespeare and poetry may also be used as part of the assessment for English Literature.

Unit 4: Coursework

You need to produce *one* or more pieces of writing designed to **explore**, **imagine** or **entertain**.

This is worth 10% of the total marks for English.

You also need to produce *two* pieces of writing, one each based on your study of:

- a play by Shakespeare
- a collection of poetry.

This is worth 10% of the total marks for English (5% each task).

The particular skills (**Assessment objectives**) involved in this Unit are listed below.

When you write your piece, you will need to:

- ✔ write clearly and imaginatively
- ✔ develop and use a wide and expressive vocabulary
- ✔ appeal to and interest your readers
- ✔ organise your writing into sentences and paragraphs
- ✔ use different kinds of sentences to achieve particular effects
- ✔ spell and punctuate your work accurately.

Each reading task will require you to:

- ✔ read and respond closely to the texts
- ✔ understand and comment on the meanings of your texts
- ✔ discuss the ways the writers have used language to convey meanings and achieve effects.

In this Unit, we will focus on the skills and approaches required for both the exam and the coursework options.

Writing to explore, imagine and entertain

In your examination and your coursework you will be given the task of producing a piece of writing that **explores**, **imagines** and/or **entertains**.

As with any other piece of writing, you will need to take care to write accurately, clearly and in an appropriate style.

However, you also need to practise some of the particular skills associated with writing to explore, imagine or entertain. In this section, we will make clear the difference between these terms, but, as you will discover, there are many similarities and overlap between them. Although the activities in this section will focus on each of the three elements separately, in the exam question or coursework task it is possible that two or more elements will be combined. The specimen paper and coursework advice at the end of this Unit will show how this works in practice.

Imaginative writing

We use language for many different purposes. Often, we use it simply as a way of exchanging and analysing information, but thankfully it can be more fun than this. We can use language to invent imaginary worlds, characters and stories. It can make us scared, or make us laugh, or make us cry; it can show us something about our own lives and experience, or it can put us in touch with the experiences of people very different from ourselves.

Imaginative writing does not just encompass short stories or novels; it can also be found in:

- writing about people: biography and autobiography
- writing from experience
- creative writing
- narratives told through letters and diaries
- writing for younger readers
- humour
- poetry
- drama scripts
- entertaining articles.

A sense of place: description, the senses and atmosphere

First we'll try to develop some ways of using language to create a sense of a particular place.

 **ACTIVITY 1**

1 Choose a place that you know well, or that you have recently visited. It may be one of your favourite places, or a place that you dislike.

2 In pairs, take it in turns to describe to each other your chosen place in as much detail as you can. In particular, you should talk about:

- what the place looks like and what you can see (colours, shapes, features, etc.)
- what sounds you can hear (voices, music, sounds either in the place itself or coming from outside – or even that very rare thing, absolute silence)
- what smells there are (even air has a smell)
- what sensations of touch there are (temperature, dryness or dampness, the texture of whatever you are standing or sitting on, etc.)
- what tastes you associate with the place.

3 As you listen to your partner's description, remember as many details as you can. When you have both finished, check your listening and memory skills by telling your partner as much as you can remember about their description.

4 Now write down your description, following the same sequence: sights, sounds, smells, touch, taste.

Sometimes you may want to do more than just capture an impression of a place – for example, you may wish to create a particular mood or atmosphere. The following extract is the opening of Philip Pullman's novel *The Amber Spyglass*, part of a trilogy entitled *His Dark Materials*.

In a valley shaded with rhododendrons, close to the snow line, where a stream milky with melt-water splashed and where doves and linnets flew among the immense pines, lay a cave, half-hidden by the crag above and the stiff heavy leaves that clustered below.

The woods were full of sound: the stream between the rocks, the wind among the needles of the pine branches, the chitter of insects and the cries of small arboreal mammals, as well as the bird-song; and from time to time a stronger gust of wind would make one of the branches of a cedar or a fir move against another and groan like a cello.

It was a place of brilliant sunlight, never undappled; shafts of lemon-gold brilliance lanced down to the forest floor between bars and pools of brown-green shade; and the light was never still, never constant, because drifting mist would often float

Continues on page 116.

among the tree-tops, filtering all the sunlight to a pearly sheen and brushing every pine-cone with moisture that glistened when the mist lifted. Sometimes the wetness in the clouds condensed into tiny drops half-mist and half-rain, that floated downwards rather than fell, making a soft rustling patter among the millions of needles.

There was a narrow path beside the stream, which led from a village – little more than a cluster of herdsmen's dwellings – at the foot of the valley, to a half-ruined shrine near the glacier at its head, a place where faded silken flags streamed out in the perpetual winds from the high mountains, and offerings of barley-cakes and dried tea were placed by pious villagers. An odd effect of the light, and the ice, and the vapour enveloped the head of the valley in perpetual rainbows.

From *The Amber Spyglass* by Philip Pullman

 **ACTIVITY 2**

Read carefully the extract from *The Amber Spyglass* that starts on page 115.

1 Consider how the extract appeals to the different senses. List some examples of description that appeal to your sight, hearing, smell, touch, taste.

2 Which of the words below do you think best describe the atmosphere created by the extract?

✦ tense	✦ tranquil	✦ exciting	✦ happy	✦ sinister
✦ delightful	✦ safe	✦ uneasy	✦ depressing	✦ restless
✦ mysterious	✦ heavenly			

3 Working in groups, copy the table below. Look at the list of devices used to create the effects you have noted. Place the devices in a rank order in importance, where (1) is the *most* important and (6) is the *least* important in creating those effects. Use the 'Comment' column to explain your decisions.

Devices	Rank order	Comment
Use of long descriptive sentences		
References to the weather		
Appeal to the different senses		
Use of **adjectives**: 'immense', 'undappled', 'lemon-gold', 'brown-green', 'pearly'		
Use of **nouns**: 'rhododendrons', 'doves', 'linnets', 'sunlight'		
Use of **verbs**: 'shaded', 'groan', 'lanced', 'floated'		

4 Now imagine the same place at a different season and/or time of day. Rewrite the description using appropriate vocabulary.

5 What words would you use to describe the atmosphere you have now created?

You can achieve some good effects in imaginative writing not just by using lots of descriptive language, as in *The Amber Spyglass*, but also by thinking about how to vary your sentence structure.

ACTIVITY 3

1 Look at the following two drafts of a piece of writing by Alan, a student. What are the differences between them and the moods they create?

> *First draft*
> The wind blew and made the leaves rustle in the trees and the branches creak, but the birds fell silent. I began to feel rather tense as I heard a dog barking somewhere and felt the first heavy drops of rain, as I knew this meant night was coming.

> *Second draft*
> The wind blew. It rustled the leaves in the trees. Branches creaked. Birds fell silent. Somewhere a dog was barking. The first heavy drops of rain fell. Night was coming.

2 Now, working in pairs, take a story that you already know, such as the fairy tale *Goldilocks and the Three Bears*. Divide the story into two episodes:

   a Where Goldilocks is in the bears' house. Your aim is to create a feeling of tension.

   b The return of the bears. Your aim is to create a sense of the panic when they discover Goldilocks in bed!

Each of you write a version of both episodes. One of you should use very short sentences, the other use longer sentences. Then discuss your two versions to see which episode worked best in which version.

ACTIVITY 4

Now practise using language to create a specific mood or atmosphere while at the same time conveying a clear impression of a particular place. In the table below there is a list of locations and a list of moods. Take a die and throw twice: the first number you throw determines the location you will describe and the second number tells you the kind of mood or atmosphere you should aim to suggest.

Golden rule: if trying to create a tense atmosphere, you do not have to use the word 'tense': let your description do the job for you! Try to avoid using any of the words listed with each mood.

Location	Mood/atmosphere
1 A street late at night	**1** Happy and optimistic Words to avoid: happy, hopeful, optimistic, jolly, good
2 A shopping centre	**2** Tense, nervous Words to avoid: tense, nervous, anxious, on edge, worried, stressed
3 A railway station	**3** Miserable, depressing Words to avoid: miserable, depressing, fed up, boring, bored
4 Inside an old house	**4** Hectic, lively Words to avoid: hectic, lively, full of life, energy, energetic
5 Somewhere in the countryside	**5** Spooky, frightening Words to avoid: spooky, frightening, scary, afraid, terrifying
6 A graveyard	**6** Exciting Words to avoid: exciting, brilliant, heart-stopping, awesome, fantastic

Autobiography

When you write to entertain, it is a good idea to start by writing about yourself. You may not have to imagine very much, but you will need to explore some of your experiences and make them entertaining for others to read about.

To begin, think about an incident from your past that you can remember quite clearly. This might be because:

- it was a particular achievement or something special
- it was either a very painful or a very enjoyable experience
- it taught you a lesson
- it changed the way you see things.

As an example, read the following extract from *My Left Foot* by Christy Brown. Here the author describes the first time he remembers using a piece of chalk to write – no mean feat, because Christy was born severely handicapped as a result of cerebral palsy.

Inside, all the family were gathered round the big kitchen fire that lit up the little room with a warm glow and made giant shadows dance on the walls and ceiling.

In a corner Mona and Paddy were sitting huddled together, a few torn school primers before them. They were writing down little sums on to an old chipped slate, using a bright piece of yellow chalk. I was close to them, propped up by a few pillows against the wall, watching.

It was the chalk that attracted me so much. It was a long, slender stick of vivid yellow. I had never seen anything like it before, and it showed up so well against the black surface of the slate that I was fascinated by it as much as if it had been a stick of gold.

Suddenly I wanted desperately to do what my sister was doing. Then – without thinking or knowing exactly what I was doing, I reached out and took the stick of chalk out of my sister's hand – *with my left foot*.

I do not know why I used my left foot to do this. It is a puzzle to many people as well as to myself, for, although I had displayed a curious interest in my toes at an early age, I had never attempted before this to use either of my feet in any way. They could have been as useless to me as were my hands. That day, however, my left foot, apparently of its own volition, reached out and very impolitely took the chalk out of my sister's hand.

I held it tightly between my toes, and, acting on an impulse, made a wild sort of scribble with it on the slate. Next moment I stopped, a bit dazed, surprised, looking down at the stick of yellow chalk stuck between my toes, not knowing what to do with it next, hardly knowing how it got there. Then I looked up and became aware that everyone had stopped talking and were staring at me silently. Nobody stirred. Mona, her black curls framing her chubby little face, stared at me with great big eyes and open mouth. Across the open hearth, his face lit by flames, sat my father, leaning forward, hands outspread on his knees, his shoulders tense. I felt the sweat break out on my forehead.

My mother came in from the pantry with a steaming pot in her hand. She stopped midway between the table and the fire, feeling the tension flowing through the room. She followed their stare and saw me, in the corner. Her eyes looked from my face down to my foot, with the chalk gripped between my toes. She put down the pot.

Then she crossed over to me and knelt down beside me, as she had done so many times before.

'I'll show you what to do with it, Chris,' she said, very slowly and in a queer, jerky way, her face flushed as if with some inner excitement.

Taking another piece of chalk from Mona, she hesitated, and then very deliberately drew, on the floor in front of me, *the single letter 'A'*.

'Copy that,' she said, looking steadily at me. 'Copy it, Christy.'

I couldn't.

I looked about me, looked around at the faces that were turned towards me, tense, excited faces that were at that moment frozen, immobile, eager, waiting for a miracle in their midst.

The stillness was profound. The room was full of flame and shadow that danced before my eyes and lulled my taut nerves into a sort of waking sleep. I could hear the sound of the water-tap dripping in the pantry, the loud ticking of the clock on the mantelshelf, and the soft hiss and crackle of the logs on the open hearth.

I tried again. I put out my foot and made a wild jerking stab with the chalk which produced a very crooked line and nothing more. Mother held the slate steady for me.

'Try again, Chris,' she whispered in my ear. 'Again.'

I did. I stiffened my body and put my left foot out again, for the third time. I drew one side of the letter. I drew half the other side. Then the stick of chalk broke and I was left with a stump. I wanted to fling it away and give up. Then I felt my mother's hand on my shoulder. I tried once more. Out went my foot. I shook, I sweated and strained every muscle. My hands were so tightly clenched that my fingernails bit into the flesh. I set my teeth so hard that I nearly pierced my lower lip. Everything in the room swam, till the faces around me were mere patches of white. But – I drew it – *the letter 'A'*. There it was on the floor before me. Shaky, with awkward, wobbly sides and a very uneven centre line. But it *was* the letter 'A'. I looked up. I saw my mother's face for a moment, tears on her cheeks. Then my father stooped down and hoisted me on to his shoulder.

I had done it! It had started – the thing that was to give my mind its chance of expressing itself. True, I couldn't speak with my lips, but now I would speak through something more lasting than spoken words – written words.

From *My Left Foot* by Christy Brown

ACTIVITY 5

Work in groups to discuss the extract from *My Left Foot*.

1   Explain why the incident in the extract was important to Christy Brown.

2   Suggest how you think this incident changed his life.

3   Pick out the parts of the extract where Christy creates a sense of tension.

4   Pick out those phrases that convey how much of a struggle it was for Christy to write the letter 'A'.

ACTIVITY 6

Work in groups.

1 First think about a memory you have of an incident that in some way brought about change in your life. Some examples might be:

- your first meeting with an important person in your life
- moving house
- first day at a new school
- passing or failing a test
- learning to ride a bike
- getting into trouble
- saying goodbye to a close friend or relative.

2 Jot down the bare outline of the incident. One example, by a student called Julie, is given below.

One thing I remember is when I was at primary school. I had this teacher that I really hated. She was very strict and seemed always to pick on me. Then one day I had an accident in the playground. I was knocked over and I remember hurting my arm really badly. It turned out it was broken. When I was taken into school my teacher, Mrs Johnson, was there. She must have been good at first aid because she seemed to know straight away that I'd hurt it pretty badly. She looked after me just like my mum would, and when the ambulance came, went with me to hospital. She held my hand and tried to make me smile even though it was really hurting. She stayed with me until my mum came, and I saw a completely different side to her. We seemed to get on fine after that.

ACTIVITY 6 (continued)

3 Now think about the sequence of events. There are many ways we can arrange the events in a story. The most obvious is to start at the beginning – and end at the end. But there are alternatives! For example, you could start at the end and tell the story in a flashback.

Copy the table below. Decide the sequence that you think works best for the events in Julie's story. Then do the same for your own incident.

4 Each part of the story could be told differently. As a writer, you might decide to use:

a straightforward narration – you tell the story

b direct speech – you quote exactly what the people in the story say to each other

c a mixture of these.

For the different parts of Julie's story listed in the table, decide whether method **a**, **b** or **c** would work best, and make a note of the reasons for your choice.

Part of story	Preferred sequence	Best method	Reasons
A scene in the classroom when Julie felt Mrs Johnson was unkind to her			
The scene when Mrs Johnson sees Julie's injury			
The scene in the playground when Julie falls over			
The meeting of Julie's mum with Julie and Mrs Johnson in the hospital			
Julie tells us about how her ideas about Mrs Johnson were changed by what happened and what she had learned from the incident			
Mrs Johnson comforts Julie in the ambulance			

5 Finally, write a full account of your own memorable incident.

Characters

Once you have tried writing about yourself, try writing about other people – either real or imaginary. There are a number of methods you can use to create characters:

- **describe** their appearance and movement
- **describe** their habits, likes and dislikes
- **narrate** their actions, choosing **verbs** and **adverbs** carefully to convey precisely their personal way of doing things
- **reported speech** (e.g. *She said that she was pleased.*)
- **direct speech**, trying to capture their personality in the way they speak (e.g. *'I'm so pleased!' she exclaimed with a smile*).

When doing any of these things, choosing *precisely* the right words you need to convey the desired impression is very important – as we shall see. By way of example, we'll look at how J. R. R. Tolkien introduces the character of Strider in *The Fellowship of the Ring*, the first volume of *The Lord of the Rings*.

Suddenly Frodo noticed that a strange-looking (1) ………… man sitting in the shadows near the wall, was also listening intently to the hobbit-talk. He had a tall tankard in front of him, and was smoking a long-stemmed pipe (2) ………… carved. His legs were stretched out before him, showing high boots of supple leather that fitted him well, but had seen much wear and were now caked with mud. A (3) ………… cloak of heavy dark-green cloth was drawn close about him, and in spite of the heat of the room he wore a hood that (4) ………… his face; but the (5) …………… of his eyes could be seen as he watched the hobbits.

'Who is that?' Frodo asked, when he got a chance to whisper to Mr Butterbur. 'I don't think you introduced him?'

'Him?' said the landlord in an answering whisper, cocking an eye without turning his head. 'I don't rightly know. He is one of the wandering folk – Rangers we call them. He seldom (6) …………: not but what he can tell a rare tale when he has the mind. He disappears for a month, or a year, and then he pops up again. …

Frodo found that Strider was now (7) ………… at him, as if he had heard or guessed all that had been said. Presently, with a (8) ………… and a nod, he invited Frodo to come over and sit by him. As Frodo drew near he threw back his hood, showing a (9) …………, and in a pale (10) ………… face a pair of (11) ………… eyes.

'I am called Strider,' he said in a (12) ………… voice.

From *The Fellowship of the Ring* by J. R. R. Tolkien

 ACTIVITY 7

Read the extract above. The numbered gaps indicate words or phrases that have been omitted.

1 Copy the table below and note examples of the methods Tolkien uses to convey impressions of Strider.

Method	Examples
Description: appearance and movement	
Description: habits, likes and dislikes	
Narration of actions: verbs and adverbs	
Reported speech	
Direct speech	

ACTIVITY 7 (continued)

2 For each of the missing words or phrases numbered (1)–(12) in the extract, there are various suggestions listed below. Working in groups, discuss the *different* impressions of Strider that would be created by these suggestions.

  (1) strikingly handsome/weather-beaten/fat and ugly/friendly-looking

  (2) curiously/crudely/neatly/elaborately/beautifully

  (3) spotless/expensive-looking/travel-stained/tatty/grubby

  (4) framed/totally obscured/enclosed/overshadowed/revealed

  (5) glint/gleam/whites/dark fire/flicker

  (6) talks/drinks/fights/swears/eats

  (7) glaring/staring/looking/pointing/leering

  (8) angry gesture/wag of a finger/wave of his hand

  (9) shaggy head of dark hair flecked with grey/shiny bald head with traces of stubble/long mane of soft shiny hair

(10) stern/gaunt/rugged/scarred/blotchy

(11) keen grey/smouldering dark/gentle blue/intense green

(12) high-pitched/low/gravelly/smooth/croaky

(You can find the actual words/phrases used by Tolkien at the bottom of this page.)

ACTIVITY 8

Imagine you are writing a story in which you need to introduce two characters for the first time. Write two passages, one for each character, in which you aim to convey an impression of his/her character and personality as vividly as possible.

Some useful words and phrases for this section

Past tense	First and third person pronouns	Dialogue	Metaphor	Simile

You can make your writing for this section effective by:

- writing in the past tense
- using either a first or a third person narrator: *I was waiting …*, *She was waiting …*, but be consistent
- using dialogue sparingly but effectively, and carefully choosing the verbs to introduce it: *asked, begged, demanded,* etc.
- using descriptive language such as metaphors and similes but make sure that the ones you use are original and interesting.

The actual words/phrases used by Tolkien are given below, upside down.

(1) weather-beaten; (2) curiously; (3) travel-stained; (4) overshadowed; (5) gleam; (6) talks; (7) looking; (8) wave of his hand; (9) shaggy head of dark hair flecked with grey; (10) stern; (11) keen grey; (12) low.

Part 1: Response to Shakespeare

In this part of your course, you will study a play by Shakespeare and are required to produce a written response to it.

You need to think carefully about the impact the play has on an audience, and about how it reflects the time when it was written.

The Examination Board suggests a couple of alternative plays for the Unit 3 examination, but the activities that follow are based on *Much Ado About Nothing*, which is set for examination from 2003 until at least June 2006. This play can just as easily be used as the basis for the coursework option. The kinds of activities suggested here can also be applied to *Romeo and Juliet* or any other Shakespeare play you study.

The same texts may be studied and similar passages set for comment at both Foundation and Higher Tier. However, the tasks set and the quality of work expected are different.

A prologue: the wedding of the year

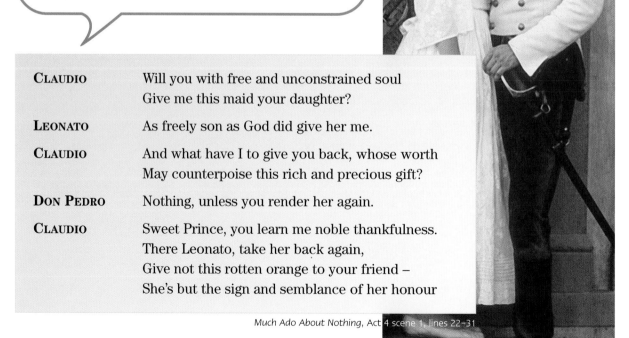

Imagine the scene. You are awaiting the society wedding of the year. It is the big day for the young Count Claudio and the lovely Hero, the Becks and Posh Spice of their day. You have taken your place in the church. The remainder of the guests are quietly waiting. The bride, looking beautiful, shyly glances towards her beloved husband to be. He in turn speaks to the bride's father, Leonato. The Prince himself, Don Pedro, looks on. You wait for the anticipated words to be spoken.

Then, this:

CLAUDIO	Will you with free and unconstrained soul Give me this maid your daughter?
LEONATO	As freely son as God did give her me.
CLAUDIO	And what have I to give you back, whose worth May counterpoise this rich and precious gift?
DON PEDRO	Nothing, unless you render her again.
CLAUDIO	Sweet Prince, you learn me noble thankfulness. There Leonato, take her back again, Give not this rotten orange to your friend – She's but the sign and semblance of her honour

Much Ado About Nothing, Act 4 scene 1, lines 22–31

What is going on? You can hardly believe your ears and eyes; but yes, it's true. The bridegroom, the well-liked war hero Claudio, has accused his bride, Hero, of being unfaithful to him, and has shamed her in front of the whole church! No, he will *not* take her to be his lawful wedded wife! Hero faints; Claudio rages. How *could* she sleep with someone else the night before the wedding?! Hero's friend and cousin Beatrice runs to her side; Claudio's friend Benedick watches from the sidelines, unsure what to do. Now even Hero's father Leonato joins in. How *dare* she bring such shame to the family?!

The priest panics and the ceremony disintegrates into chaos. The other guests are starting to disperse. You had better go.

This dramatic scene occurs about halfway through *Much Ado About Nothing* by William Shakespeare. In our exploration of the play we will find out who these people are, how they got into this mess, and what happens next.

The play, the man, the theatre

Shakespeare's 37 plays are usually classified as **Tragedies** (such as *Romeo and Juliet*, *Macbeth*), **History** plays (such as *Richard III*, *Henry V*), **Romances** (such as *The Tempest*) or **Comedies** (such as *A Midsummer Night's Dream* and our play, *Much Ado About Nothing*).

Each of these types of play (or **genres**) tends to follow similar patterns and share certain characteristics. So what are Comedies like, and what can we expect from *Much Ado About Nothing*?

 **ACTIVITY 1**

Work in groups. Which of the following would you expect to find in a play that is described as a 'Comedy'? Tick the appropriate boxes in the table below.

Feature	Tick	Feature	Tick
Someone dying		A love story	
A serious message or theme		A serious argument	
Lots of jokes		An evil, vicious character	
A scene in a cemetery		Funny characters	
A wedding		A scene like the one above	
Insults and abuse		A happy ending	

You probably didn't tick *all* of these – perhaps you thought some of them sounded more like a Tragedy! As you get to know the story of *Much Ado*, it will be interesting to return to this table later.

Much Ado About Nothing was probably written and first performed around 1598. It has always been among the most popular of Shakespeare's plays and 400 years on is still regularly performed today. Perhaps the best-known recent version is the film made by Kenneth Branagh in 1993.

Drama and Shakespeare's theatre

Much Ado was first enjoyed by audiences at the original Globe theatre in London. The theatre Shakespeare wrote for was rather different from most modern theatres. This was because:

- all performances were in the daylight, and in the open air
- many of the audience stood to watch and listen to the play
- the audience were very close to the action, and surrounded the stage on three sides
- there was little scenery
- all the actors were either men or boys (who took the female roles).

Nowadays, you can see *Much Ado* on film or video, in a modern theatre with lighting, scenery and comfortable seats – or perhaps more like Shakespeare first imagined it, in the newly reconstructed Globe in London.

Wherever you see *Much Ado*, or even if you don't have the chance of doing so while you are studying it, always remember that it is a **play** on the **stage** intended to be acted for an **audience**. These three words should always figure frequently in anything you write about Shakespeare.

For this reason, from now on we will refer to the text of the play as a **script**.

Who's who in *Much Ado*

 ACTIVITY 2

Work in groups. Consider the descriptions of the main characters listed below. For each one, suggest an actor that you think would be suitable to cast in the part. You might find it helpful to flick through a copy of the *TV Times* or a film magazine as you do this.

Character	Suggested actor
Don Pedro, the Prince of Aragon A mature, dignified, noble well-brought-up man	
Don John, Don Pedro's bastard brother In Shakespeare's time, illegitimate children were viewed with suspicion and often stereotyped as evil and scheming. Don John is no exception – the main source of evil in the play	
Claudio, a young lord of Florence A handsome young man who has recently won praise for his heroism in the wars	
Benedick, a young lord of Padua A slightly older, more cynical man than Claudio – known for his sarcastic humour and his determination never to marry	
Hero A pretty but rather quiet young girl with whom Claudio falls in love	
Beatrice, Hero's cousin Much more confident, witty and sharp-tongued than Hero. She and Benedick always seem to insult and abuse each other whenever they meet	
Leonato, Hero's father The respectable middle-aged Governor of Messina	
Antonio, Leonato's older brother Now an old man	
Dogberry A foolish and rather ignorant man who is in charge of the 'Watch', the Elizabethan equivalent of the local police	

The plot of *Much Ado*

As you start to read the script of *Much Ado About Nothing*, you may find it useful to refer to this simple summary of the main points in the development of the story.

> I will assume thy part in some disguise,
> And tell fair Hero I am Claudio, ...

The young men of Messina return after a successful campaign in war. Claudio falls in love with Hero but, being shy, asks his friend Don Pedro to talk to her for him.

> 'Tis certain so; the Prince woos for himself.

The masqued party that night provides the opportunity – but Claudio becomes convinced that Don Pedro has pursued Hero for himself, a view stirred up by the wicked Don John.

> Lady, as you are mine, I am yours; ...

Luckily, the misunderstanding is cleared up and Hero and Claudio become engaged.

> 'Against my will I am sent to bid you come in to dinner' – there's a double meaning in that.

Convinced and shamed, Benedick now sees Beatrice with new eyes!

> What fire is in mine ears?
> Can this be true?

Hero and her maid Ursula perform a similar trick on Beatrice, with similar results ...

> ... the lady is disloyal.

Claudio's amusement at Benedick's new love now is cut short by Don John's shocking allegation.

> Come bid me do anything for thee.
>
> Kill Claudio.

Benedick declares his love for Beatrice and accepts Hero's innocence. He will do anything for Beatrice, he says – she challenges him to 'Kill Claudio'.

> You are a villain – I jest not. I will make it good how you dare, with what you dare, and when you dare.

As the Friar suggested, it has been announced that Hero is dead. Antonio and Leonato grieve and now believe in her innocence. First they, and then Benedick, challenge Claudio.

> ... My brother hath a daughter,
> Almost the copy of my child that's dead, ...

Meanwhile Conrade and Borachio are finally brought to justice and Don John's plan is exposed. Don John has fled, Claudio and Don Pedro seek forgiveness and Claudio now agrees to marry a 'cousin' of Hero whom he has never seen.

"If we can do this, Cupid is no longer an archer; his glory shall be ours, for we are the only love-gods."

Meanwhile, Benedick and Beatrice have been insulting each other as usual. Leonato, Pedro and the rest decide to try to trick them into love.

"Grow this to what adverse issue it can, I will put it in practice."

However, Borachio gives his master Don John a cunning plan to spoil the mood with a trick of his own – fooling Claudio into believing Hero is seeing someone else.

"What was it you told me of today, that your niece Beatrice was in love with Signor Benedick?"

Knowing Benedick to be eavesdropping, Don Pedro and co now let him hear them say that Beatrice loves him.

"... partly by the dark night, which did deceive them, but chiefly by my villainy, which did confirm any slander that Don John had made, away went Claudio enraged; ..."

Don John's servant Borachio boasts to his friend Conrade of their cruel trick – pretending that a serving girl seen at his window last night was actually Hero. The set-up was witnessed by Claudio and Don Pedro.

"Marry sir our watch tonight ... ha' t'en a couple of as arrant knaves as any in Messina."

Luckily, a member of Dogberry's 'Watch' overhears and arrests Borachio and Conrade – but Leonato is too busy to listen when they try to tell him.

"O on my soul my cousin is belied!"

At the wedding, Hero is publicly accused of being unfaithful with Borachio. She collapses, and her furious father sides with the men. Beatrice is convinced of her innocence, and the Friar comes up with a plan.

"Done to death by slanderous tongues
Was the Hero that here lies; ..."

The men pay their respects at Hero's tomb.

"Peace, I will stop your mouth."

The real Hero is brought forth and, to everyone's delight and amazement, unmasked. She is reunited with Claudio and all is revealed, also, about Benedick and Beatrice.

"Strike up pipers."

All of Messina celebrate a double marriage with singing and dancing. The play ends with the news that Don John has been recaptured.

 **ACTIVITY 3**

Work in groups.

1   For each of the moments in the story outlined on pages 128–129, create your own tableaux or 'frozen moments'. Check carefully with the script to find out which characters are present, and where the scene is taking place.

2   Consider which of these characters you would blame most for the suffering and humiliation that Hero faces: Don John, Borachio, Claudio, Don Pedro, Leonato, Margaret or Dogberry. Place the characters in a rank order of importance, saying which of them is the *most* to blame (1) and which is the *least* to blame (7).

3   Look back to your work in Activity 1 on the subject of Comedy (page 125). Are there any of the features that you didn't think belonged in a Comedy that you have now found in *Much Ado*?

What makes good drama?

As you get to know the characters and plot of *Much Ado*, start to think about it from a dramatic point of view.

 **ACTIVITY 4**

In the table below is a list of features that tend to make for interesting drama, whether it be soap opera on the television or plays acted on stage. Working in groups, copy the table and for each feature, say:

● whether you agree that it *is* important in a drama

● where you can find an example of that feature in your studied script.

Dramatic feature	Agree?	Examples
Characters come into conflict with each other		
Some characters face difficult problems		
There are some intense, emotional moments		
There is some contrast between moments of tension and humour		
Has a message or raises some serious issues		

Themes and issues

As with the stories you studied in Unit 2, it is important not just to understand and follow the story the play tells, but also to begin to think about the kinds of issues or themes Shakespeare explores in his plays. As you become familiar with the script you are studying, you can use the following activity as a starting point for your discussion of *Much Ado About Nothing*.

If you are studying an alternative text, you will need to carry out some similar investigations.

ACTIVITY 5

Work in groups to discuss the following.

1 **A man thing?**

Consider the behaviour and attitudes of the men in the play towards women and marriage.

● How do the men differ from each other in their behaviour and attitudes? How might men today behave?

● Look at the way the men in the play condemn Hero. What is your response to the language they use ('this rotten orange', 'a common stale'), and their willingness to believe the worst of Hero?

● Even if Hero had been guilty, do you think their behaviour is justified?

● When Beatrice challenges Benedick to 'Kill Claudio', what decisions was she forcing him to make? Do you think it was a fair thing for her to demand?

● At the end, Claudio and Hero end up 'happy ever after'. Do you think Claudio has learned his lesson, and does he deserve his Hero?

2 **A question of love**

Compare and contrast the two pairs of lovers, Beatrice and Benedick and Hero and Claudio.

● How did the two pairs come to fall in love with each other? Which of the couples do you think has the stronger marriage?

● What do you think Shakespeare might be suggesting in the play about love and marriage?

3 **Tricks and deceptions**

Many of the twists in the plot are based on the difference between the appearances of things and the reality – and the inability of some characters to tell them apart.

● List the various tricks, deceptions, lies and misunderstandings that occur in the play.

● Which of them lead to comical, and which to more serious consequences?

● Which characters emerge as the wisest, and the most able to perceive the truth about people and things?

Much Ado in context: love and marriage, then and now

Modern audiences still enjoy *Much Ado* and the fun and games that accompany Claudio and Hero, and Benedick and Beatrice, on their way to wedded bliss. However, ideas about love and marriage have changed since the sixteenth century. In the examination, you need to show that you have thought about some of these changes.

When Shakespeare wrote his play, it was very common for marriages to be arranged. It was important for wealthy and powerful families to make suitable matches. It was not unusual, then, for young people to become engaged and get married without really having the chance to get to know – and trust – each other properly.

Daughters were often seen as a financial burden; they were expected to present their future father-in-law with a cash dowry when they married. If they married well, however, they would be provided for for the rest of their lives. Most women were unable to earn money or own property themselves. It was very important that women were thought to be virgins when they married; a family's honour depended on it.

Shakespeare and other writers of that time were certainly interested in the possibility of marriages based on romantic love. Many of Shakespeare's plays, especially Comedies such as *Much Ado*, *As You Like It* and *Twelfth Night*, seem to ask the question, 'what is the best basis for true love and a happy marriage?'.

 **ACTIVITY 6**

Work in groups. Think about the aspects of the plot of *Much Ado* listed in the table below. How might the responses of a sixteenth-century audience and a modern audience differ? Copy the table and note your ideas.

Aspect of *Much Ado*	Different responses
Leonato seems to want to 'marry off' Beatrice	
Hero seems to agree to marry Claudio without even meeting him	
Beatrice seems determined not to marry anyone because she has not met a man she can love and respect	
Hero's own father turns violently against his daughter because of the dishonour she brings on him	

Shakespeare's language

The language of Shakespeare can seem rather strange and even off-putting at first, but most people find it is worth the effort because of the extraordinary things he does with words in his plays.

Shakespeare's language is different from what we are used to today for a number of reasons.

- Some of the words he uses have either changed meanings or are only used rarely nowadays, so we no longer (for example) use the words 'thee' and 'thou' (unless you live in parts of Yorkshire).
- The grammar of English has changed since Shakespeare was alive.
- He sometimes refers to things that are no longer part of our everyday lives.
- As a poet, Shakespeare's language is rich in similes, metaphors and imagery.
- Sometimes his sentences can seem complex because the words follow a word order that is different from modern English.

A good edition of the play you are studying should help you with most of the difficult words and phrases – and you don't need to understand every word to achieve a good grade in your GCSE examination. However, you do need to be able to follow the gist of a scene and to comment on some examples of Shakespeare's use of language – especially his use of similes, metaphors and images.

 Verse and prose

Shakespeare uses a mixture of verse (poetry) and prose in his plays. It is usually easy to see which is which; the verse does not often rhyme (this verse is called blank verse), except sometimes at the very end of a scene, but is set out like poetry, as in this speech of Leonato's after he hears Claudio accuse his daughter, Hero, of being unfaithful:

> Wherefore? Why, doth not every earthly thing
> Cry shame upon her? Could she here deny
> The story that is printed in her blood?
> Do not live Hero, do not ope thine eyes.
> For did I think thou wouldst not quickly die,
> Thought I thy spirits were stronger than thy shames,
> Myself would on the rearward of reproaches
> Strike at thy life.

Act 4 scene 1, lines 118–125

At other times, the lines are written in continuous prose, as in these lines spoken by Dogberry when he is accusing Conrade and Borachio:

> Marry sir, they have committed false report; moreover they
> have spoken untruths; secondarily, they are slanders; sixth
> and lastly, they have belied a lady; thirdly, they have verified
> unjust things; and to conclude, they are lying knaves.

Act 5 scene 1, lines 203–207

Verse and prose (continued)

Why does Shakespeare decide to write in verse in one place and prose somewhere else? The answer is not always straightforward but we can sum up the general rule as follows:

Verse: used by higher status characters

used in dramatic, emotional or important scenes

Prose: used by lower status or less important characters

used in lighter or more comical scenes

used at moments when the tension is relaxed, to contrast with the verse

The iambic pentameter

When you write in verse, most of the lines will generally follow a similar rhythmic pattern – you can hear the same pattern in modern English sentences such as:

I'm **go**ing **home** and **stay**ing **in** all **night**

My **fav**ourite **food** is **pi**zza, **beans** and **chips**

U**ni**ted **scored** a **brill**iant **goal** last **night**

The pattern usually consists of five beats or stresses evenly spaced in a line of ten syllables. It is called an **iambic pentameter** as 'pentameter' means five beats and an 'iamb' is a technical term for a pair of unstressed and stressed syllables.

Try creating some of your own iambic pentameters based on what you did yesterday evening. Beat out the rhythm with a pencil to check you are getting the beats in the right places.

Looking closely at a scene

Let's now turn to the scene we started with, at the beginning of this section (page 124) – the wedding of Hero where Claudio and Don Pedro make their accusations (the start of Act 4 scene 1).

Here is a question about this passage that could equally well be asked about parts of any play you are studying:

What makes this such an important and dramatic part of the play?

 ACTIVITY 7

Working in groups, try to act out the lines on pages 135–136. As you do so, use the prompt questions beside the text to prepare to write a detailed response to the question above.

Points to remember and to discuss

- It is the script of a play.
- It takes place on a stage.
- It is performed for an audience.
- It was written at a time when some ideas and attitudes were different.
- It may relate to the play's main issues and themes.

*Enter **Don Pedro**, **Don John**, **Leonato**, **Friar Francis**,
Claudio, **Benedick**, **Hero**, **Beatrice**, and attendants.*

What will be the mood of the audience as we watch the main characters enter? What kind of a spectacle will this form on stage?

LEONATO	Come Friar Francis, be brief; only to the plain form of marriage, and you shall recount their particular duties afterwards.
FRIAR	You come hither, my lord, to marry this lady?
CLAUDIO	No.
LEONATO	To be married to her. Friar, you come to marry her.
FRIAR	Lady, you come hither to be married to this Count?
HERO	I do.
FRIAR	If either of you know any inward impediment why you should not be conjoined, I charge you on your souls, to utter it.
CLAUDIO	Know you any, Hero?
HERO	None my lord.
FRIAR	Know you any, Count?
LEONATO	I dare make his answer, None.
CLAUDIO	O what men dare do! What men may do! What men daily do, not knowing what they do!
BENEDICK	How now, interjections? Why then, some be of laughing, as, ah, ha, he!
CLAUDIO	Stand thee by, Friar. Father, by your leave – Will you with free and unconstrained soul Give me this maid your daughter?
LEONATO	As freely son as God did give her me.
CLAUDIO	And what have I to give you back, whose worth May counterpoise this rich and precious gift?
DON PEDRO	Nothing, unless you render her again.
CLAUDIO	Sweet Prince, you learn me noble thankfulness. There Leonato, take her back again, Give not this rotten orange to your friend – She's but the sign and semblance of her honour.

What is the impact of Claudio's blunt response? How do you think the other characters react? How is the mood already changing?

Leonato misunderstands Claudio here. What does he think he means?

Claudio avoids the question and confronts Hero here. What is happening to the tension levels at this point?

Any evidence here of Leonato's growing nervousness? Why is he so anxious that things go smoothly?

Benedick tries to make a joke. How is this typical of his character? Do you think anyone else laughs?

Try saying this line. How do you think Claudio says the words 'rich' and 'precious'? What does the word 'gift' suggest about how Hero is viewed?

How does Don Pedro's line connect to the title of the play? What dramatic action do you think takes place on this line?

Verse or prose? What happens to the language at this point in the scene? Why, do you think?

Comment on the impact of Claudio's words here on the other characters, and on the audience. What is your response to the image of the 'rotten orange'?

Behold how like a maid she blushes here!
O what authority and show of truth
Can cunning sin cover itself withal!
Comes not that blood as modest evidence
To witness simple virtue? Would you not swear,
All you that see her, that she were a maid
By these exterior shows? But she is none;
She knows the heat of a luxurious bed.
Her blush is guiltiness, not modesty.

LEONATO   What do you mean, my lord?

CLAUDIO   Not to be married,
Not to knit my soul to an approved wanton.

LEONATO   Dear my lord, if you in your own proof
Have vanquished the resistance of her youth,
And made defeat of her virginity –

CLAUDIO   I know what you would say. If I have known her,
You will say she did embrace me as a husband,
And so extenuate the 'forehand sin.
No, Leonato,
I never tempted her with word too large,
But, as a brother to his sister, showed
Bashful sincerity and comely love.

HERO   And seemed I ever otherwise to you?

CLAUDIO   Out on thee, seeming! I will write against it.
You seem to me as Dian in her orb,
As chaste as is the bud ere it be blown;
But you are more intemperate in your blood
Than Venus, or those pampered animals
That rage in savage sensuality.

HERO   Is my lord well that he doth speak so wide?

LEONATO   Sweet Prince, why speak not you?

DON PEDRO   What should I speak?
I stand dishonoured that have gone about
To link my dear friend to a common stale.

LEONATO   Are these things spoken, or do I but dream?

DON JOHN   Sir, they are spoken, and these things are true.

BENEDICK   This looks not like a nuptial.

HERO   True? O God!

Side questions:

What does this suggest is Hero's reaction here? Why do you think she doesn't try to defend herself?

What would be the audience's reaction to this phrase?

How does Hero's father Leonato react to these terrible accusations? What do you think of his reaction?

At last! Hero speaks! Why so silent so long? And why is the word 'seemed' unfortunate? Why does Claudio repeat it, and how does this relate to the theme of 'appearances and reality'?
Which of Claudio's words and images here convey his anger and disgust with Hero?

Why does Leonato turn to Don Pedro?

Comment on the impact of the Prince's language (a stale = a prostitute).

Why would 'honour' be such a huge issue for both Don Pedro and Leonato, here, in the sixteenth century?

Two characters now speak up who have long been silent. What do you think each of them has been doing – and thinking – all this time?

In this part of the course you will study and respond to a collection of poetry in English. If you are taking the Unit 3 examination, this will be a section from *Opening Lines*, the OCR Anthology. This is equally acceptable as a basis for coursework, though if you submit coursework for Unit 4 you may be studying an alternative collection.

All the activities that follow are based on poems from *Opening Lines*. You are also referred to *Working with Opening Worlds and Opening Lines*, the companion title to *Opening Lines*, which looks in much more detail at the poems.

The same texts may be studied and similar passages set at both Foundation and Higher Tier. However, the tasks set and the quality of work expected are different.

What makes poetry special?

We might start by asking what we *mean* by **poetry** and what makes it special?

 **ACTIVITY 8**

Work in groups to consider the ideas about poetry in the table below that a group of students has suggested. Copy the table, then:

1 Use your experience of studying the poems in your anthology to decide which of these ideas best describes what poetry *is*. Score each statement from 1 to 5 with (1) strongly agree, (5) strongly disagree and (3) not sure.

2 Note examples of poems that illustrate each point – you can add more examples as you read more poems.

Ideas about poetry	Agreement score	Examples/comment
Poems usually have a 'point' or message.		
Poems are about feelings.		
Poems use rhythm and rhyme.		
Poems are difficult to understand.		
Poems use language in unusual ways.		
There may be different meanings in a poem rather than a single 'right' way of understanding it.		
Poems are usually about death or other depressing subjects.		
Poems make you think.		
Poems use patterns.		
Poems are just pieces of ordinary language set out in lines and verses with capital letters.		
Poems are usually set out in verses or stanzas.		

There is plenty of room for disagreement and discussion here – but one thing we *can* say is that poetry is a *special* form of language – or, rather, it uses language in special or unusual ways. It is usually designed to make us think, or to make us feel something of what the writer feels about a place, person, event or situation, but can often be written just for fun.

Most of the poems you are likely to study are fairly short. Unlike stories or plays, poems usually try to say what they have to say in a few words. To do this, writers of poems work hard to **compress** their ideas and to include only essential words. It is almost as if poets take the words, ideas and feelings of everyday life, mix them together, and boil them down until they produce a very concentrated substance, which we call poetry.

So remember – poetry is **condensed** language: we have to read it in a different way (and at a different speed) from prose.

Making sense of poems

People write poems because they want to convey a feeling, an idea or an experience – so it's important always to start by getting an overall idea of what the basic meaning or point of a poem is.

When you read a poem, beware simply searching for examples of special uses of language or poetic techniques before you've enjoyed the poem for what it is. This would be like trying to work out the ingredients of a cake without allowing yourself to taste it first!

 **ACTIVITY 9**

1 Read the following poem, 'A Poison Tree', by William Blake a couple of times. As you do so, jot down any thoughts, ideas, images or feelings that occur to you – there are some suggestions to get you started.

2 Then, in groups, decide which of the comments about the poem in the table opposite you agree or disagree with. Copy the table and use the right-hand column to make a note of your reasons, and refer to specific parts of the poem that relate to the comment.

A Poison Tree

I was angry with my friend:
I told my wrath, my wrath did end.
I was angry with my foe:
I told it not, my wrath did grow.

And I water'd it in fears,
Night and morning with my tears;
And I sunned it with smiles,
And with soft deceitful wiles.

And it grew both day and night,
Till it bore an apple bright;
And my foe beheld it shine,
And he knew that it was mine,

And into my garden stole
When the night had veil'd the pole:
In the morning glad I see
My foe outstretch'd beneath the tree

William Blake (1757–1827)

Someone who is angry – with two different people?

What does this mean?

Keeps anger bottled up? Gets worse? Holds a grudge?

Comments	Agree or disagree	Reasons
It's about how someone ends up killing their enemy.		
I didn't really understand parts of this poem.		
It seems very simple, almost childish.		
There are a lot of metaphors in the poem.		
It reminds me of the story of Adam and Eve in the Bible.		
It's about what happens when you hold a grudge against someone.		
It's about how good it feels to take revenge on someone.		
It has a very regular rhythm and rhyme – it could almost be a song.		

As you begin to explore poems such as 'A Poison Tree', it may often seem that a poem can mean several different things at once. Don't worry – this is quite normal! So, when you write about a poem, don't try to claim that you have successfully found the 'right' meaning. Instead, *suggest* what you think the poem means, and back up your ideas by referring to some details in the poem.

It is possible to get a poem completely 'wrong' if we misunderstand something the writer is saying – but there will never just be one completely 'right' answer!

 **ACTIVITY 10**

After your discussion of 'A Poison Tree', write up your analysis of the poem and its meanings. You might find it helpful to use some of the phrases below.

> One thing the poet might mean is ....
> This is because the word/phrase .... suggests ....
>
> I felt/thought that the poem seemed to be about ....
> This is because in the first/second stanza ....
>
> One thing I found puzzling about the poem was ....
> On the one hand, in the opening verse, it suggests .... On the other hand, ...

Forms of poetry

Poems, like cars, come in many different shapes and sizes, but just as we can classify cars according to whether they are sports cars, 4x4s, hatchbacks or saloons, poems too can be sorted into certain common types or **forms**. When we talk about the form of a poem we are usually referring to:

- the type and number of verses or **stanzas** it has
- the **rhyming** scheme it follows (if any)
- the kind of **rhythm** it follows.

If someone sells us a hatchback car we would usually know something about what to expect in the vehicle. So, recognising the *form* of a poem can also help us know what to expect from it.

As you study the poetry in *Opening Lines* (or in any other anthology) you will come across many different traditional forms of poetry – though many modern poems don't necessarily follow any of them. However, it is useful to know about at least a couple of the most common forms – **ballads** and **sonnets**.

Ballads

One traditional form of poem is the **ballad**. A ballad is a **narrative** poem (in other words it tells a story) and will usually have a regular rhyme and rhythm, often in four-line stanzas. Ballads sometimes have a repeated chorus between each verse, and may lend themselves either to reading aloud or even being spoken or sung to music.

Nowadays, the form of the ballad lives on in many a folk or Country and Western song!

The following verses are the opening of a ballad by Thomas Hood that tells the sad story of a young girl whose boyfriend is 'pressed' or forced into becoming a sailor, and who is unable to remain faithful to him while he is away.

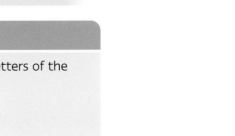

Faithless Sally Brown

Young **Ben** he **was** a **nice** young **man**,
    A **car**pen**ter** by **trade**;
And he **fell** in **love** with **Sal**ly **Brown**,
    That **was** a **la**dy's **maid**.

But as they fetch'd a walk one day,
    They met a press-gang crew;
And Sally she did faint away,
    Whilst Ben he was brought to.

The Boatswain swore with wicked words,
    Enough to shock a saint,
That though she did seem in a fit,
    'Twas nothing but a feint.

'Come girl,' said he, 'hold up your head,
    He'll be as good as me;
For when your swain is in our boat,
    A boatswain he will be.'

Thomas Hood (1799–1845)

 **ACTIVITY 11**

Many ballads were written to be read aloud. Read the verses from 'Faithless Sally Brown' out loud and, as you do so, beat out the regular rhythm using a pencil. As you do so, notice how many beats (or **stresses**) there are in each line – usually four followed by three. The use of **bold print** in the first verse of the poem should help you.

Rhyme schemes

One way of identifying the rhyming pattern of a poem is to use the letters of the alphabet to describe the sequence of rhymes at the ends of lines.

So, the pattern of 'Faithless Sally Brown' varies between:
A 'man' **B** 'trade' **C** 'Brown' **B** 'Maid' and
A 'day' **B** 'crew' **A** 'away' **B** 'to'

 **ACTIVITY 12**

Have a go at writing a ballad of your own using the same basic rhyme and rhythmic pattern as 'Faithless Sally Brown'. Start by introducing your characters and then develop the story over a number of verses.

Here are some possible starters:

Young David was a footballer
Of courage and much skill ......

There was a girl from Birmingham,
Young Tracey was her name ....

You may even be able to use your ballad as part of your coursework submission for 'Writing to explore, imagine and entertain'.

Sonnets

One of the most common traditional forms of poetry is the **sonnet**. This is a short poem – usually of 14 lines – with a regular pattern of rhymes and rhythm. As it is so short, a sonnet does not usually tell a long story as a ballad does; sonnets are more often used for exploring feelings, thoughts and emotions.

 ACTIVITY 13

1 Read the sonnet by Michael Drayton on page 143. Try doing this aloud to bring out the rhythm – again, the stresses on the first two lines are in bold print.

2 Re-read the poem and start to make your own notes about what you think the poet is saying, as you did for 'A Poison Tree' in Activity 9. There are some suggestions in the column to the right of the poem.

3 Compare your first thoughts about the poem with the short summaries below it on page 143, and decide which one fits best.

4 Now study the notes in the column to the left of the poem. With their help, decide what seem to be the rules or pattern that the sonnet follows. Think particularly about how the different parts of the *form* of the poem link to different parts of the poem's *meaning*.

Pattern	Sonnet	Meanings
First four lines – quatrain ABAB What kind of rhythmic line?	Since **there's** no **help**, come, **let** us **kiss** and **part.** Nay, **I** have **done**; you **get** no **more** of **me**; And I am glad, yea, glad with all my heart, That thus so cleanly I myself can free.	*Gives basic idea – lovers about to separate. Good thing too!*
Second quatrain – rhyme pattern of CDCD	Shake hands for ever; cancel all our vows; And when we meet at any time again, Be it not seen in either of our brows That we one jot of former love retain.	*Repeats basic idea with variations. Glad to have split up!*
Third quatrain – EFEF	Now at the last gasp of Love's latest breath, When, his pulse failing, Passion speechless lies, When Faith is kneeling by his bed of death, And Innocence is closing up his eyes;	*Another variation – or is a new image or idea to represent different feelings introduced here?*
Final couplet–GG	Now if thou would'st, when all have given him over, From death to life thou might'st him yet recover. Michael Drayton (1563–1631)	*Suddenly, a 'twist' in the tale! What is it?*

Summary A	Summary B	Summary C
Two lovers are saying goodbye. They are both glad to separate and each is looking forward to life free from the other.	Two lovers are parting and the poet is putting on an appearance of being glad – but deep down he hopes that their relationship might still be saved and they might stay together.	Two lovers are saying goodbye and are happy about it, but it is rather sad that one of them is actually dying.

Poets and language: the *what* and the *how*

When responding to and writing about a poem in your GCSE examination or coursework, you need to show that you have developed your own personal response to *what* the poet is saying, and also make some comment on *how* s/he has used language to create this response. This means pointing out the special uses of language and the interesting meanings and effects they create.

For a poet, poetic devices and special uses of language are the tools s/he uses to create a work of art and convey meanings and feelings.

Health Warning: Poetry is not for anoraks

Beware! Reading poetry is not for anoraks or train-spotters and you should avoid just 'spotting' features and devices for their own sake.

Always try to connect these technical features to the meanings and feelings in the poem.

Similes and metaphors

One of the most important items in a poet's language toolbox is the **simile** or **metaphor**. Remind yourself of how these work by looking back at Unit 2, page 75.

However, poets try to get away from phrases that are too well known (**clichés**) and by making unusual comparisons make us think about things in a new way.

ACTIVITY 14

Read the poem, 'You're' by Sylvia Plath below.

You're

Clownlike, happiest on your hands,
Feet to the stars, and moon-skulled,
Gilled like a fish. A common-sense
Thumbs-down on the dodo's mode.
Wrapped up in yourself like a spool,
Trawling your dark as owls do.
Mute as a turnip from the Fourth
Of July to All Fools' Day,
O high-riser, my little loaf.

Vague as fog and looked for like mail.
Farther off than Australia.
Bent-backed Atlas, our traveled prawn.
Snug as a bud and at home
Like a sprat in a pickle jug.
A creel of eels, all ripples.
Jumpy as a Mexican bean.
Right, like a well-done sum.
A clean slate, with your own face on.

Sylvia Plath (1932–63)

1 First, decide what Plath is actually describing in the poem.

2 Once you've solved the riddle of the poem, think about some of the comparisons Sylvia Plath makes, and how they make you think in a new way about the baby she is expecting.

3 Use a table like the one below to record your responses. Some examples have been done to get you started.

Phrase	Simile or metaphor?	What characteristics/qualities does the baby share with the subject of the comparison?
'Gilled like a fish'	Simile	Like a fish, the baby inside the womb receives oxygen without breathing
'Wrapped up ... like a spool'	Simile	Refers to the way the baby is tightly curled, like tape on a spool
'O high-riser, my little loaf'	Metaphor	Refers to the baby's gradual growth, but bread is also associated with life
'looked for like mail'		
'Snug as a bud'		
'Like a sprat in a pickle jug'		
'A creel of eels, all ripples'		

Similes and metaphors are just two of the many 'tools' in the poet's toolkit. As you study your collection of poetry, you will come across many, if not all, of the following techniques.

 Some poetic terms and techniques

Alliteration:	repeated consonant sounds, usually at the beginning of a word
	Peter Piper picked a peck of pickled pepper
Assonance:	repeating vowel sounds, but without actually rhyming
	The grave's a fine and private place
Caesura:	a break, or pause in the middle of a verse or line (shown below as*) – usually shown by punctuation
	*An expert. * He would set the wing*
	And fit the bright steel-pointed sock.
Enjambement:	where the sense (and sentence) runs on unbroken from line to line
	After lunch my daughter picked
	Handfuls of the wild flowers
	She knew her grandfather liked best
	And piled them in the basket of her bicycle ...
Iambic pentameter:	a line of (usually) ten syllables, with five stressed syllables alternating with five unstressed
	*Turn **back** to **look** ag**ain** at **Shake**speare **here**! (page 134)*
Metaphor:	an implied comparison between two different things or ideas
Onomatopoeia:	use of words whose sound actually resembles the noises they describe (may also include some alliteration)
	Snap, crack and pop! The wild wind whistles!
Personification:	a kind of metaphor that refers to objects as if they were human
Quatrain:	a set of four lines within a poem
Rhyming couplet:	a pair of successive lines that rhyme
	*Love, all alike, no season knows, nor **clime***
	*Nor hours, days, months, which are the rags of **time** ...*
Simile:	a comparison made by using the words 'like' or 'as'
Sonnet:	a short poem of 14 lines and a regular pattern of rhyme and rhythm
Stanza:	verse

Putting it all together: reading and responding to a poem

One way of approaching a poem is to concentrate first on developing your ideas about *what* the poem is saying and *what* your response to it is, and then to focus on *how* the poet has achieved this result. You may find the following plan helpful.

Step 1: First thoughts Read the poem a couple of times to get a first impression. Jot down your first thoughts and reactions.

Step 2: Making sense Jot down some more points about the main ideas or feelings the poem conveys. (Try using mind maps or spider diagrams for this.) Don't worry too much about understanding every detail at this stage.

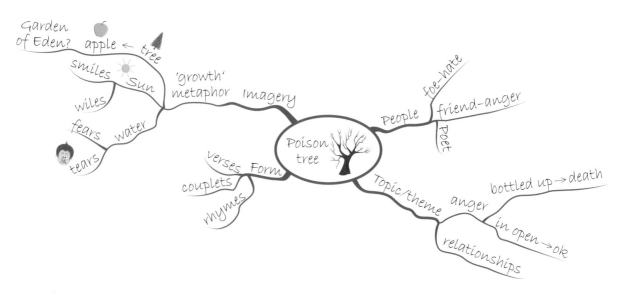

Step 3: A closer look Read the poem through more carefully. Concentrate on any difficult details. Keep adding to your notes or diagram.

Step 4: How it works Finally try to notice things about the form, structure, imagery and other uses of language in the poem. Add further to your notes or diagram.

 **ACTIVITY 15**

Now apply this method to any of the poems that you are studying for the examination or for coursework.

1 Prepare your mind map as above.

2 Using your mind map as an aid, give a short talk to your class about the poem you have studied.

3 Finally, write up your study of your poem as an essay. Take each spoke of your diagram in turn and make it the topic of a paragraph, quoting some examples from the poem to make your points about the poet's use of language.

Themes and comparisons

Whether you are doing coursework or entering the exam for this Unit (or both) you will have to do more than just write about one poem at a time. The tasks or assignments you will be given will ask you to make comparisons between two or more poems.

Comparative essays are more difficult than just writing about a single poem. They involve discussing things that the poems have in common, and also ways in which they differ.

 ACTIVITY 16

1 To decide how best to approach a comparative essay, imagine you have been asked to compare an apple and an orange. Jot down some ideas. You may come up with some of these points.

Both round

Different colours

Both fruit

Different taste

Apple has skin, orange has peel

Apples grow in the UK – not oranges

Apple skin is edible, not orange

Drinks are made from them both

Apple crunchy, orange juicy

Similar size

2 Once you have come up with your ideas, think about the best way of organising them into an essay. Choose which of the following versions you think does the job best, and suggest reasons.

Version A	Version B
Apples are fruit, usually green or red, and are round shaped. They are crunchy to eat, can taste quite sharp, have skin, which you can eat, and are grown in the UK. They are about 3 inches in diameter and can be made into a drink. Oranges are also fruit. They are orange coloured, and are usually juicy and sweet. Oranges have a peel that you can't eat, and they aren't grown in the UK. Oranges are usually around 3 inches in diameter. You can make them into a drink.	Apples and oranges have several similarities. They are both round fruit of similar size, and can be made into a drink. However, they also differ in some ways. Whereas apples are grown in the UK, oranges are grown abroad. What's more, the peel of oranges is inedible, whereas we can eat apple skin. Obviously apples and oranges are of different colour, and while apples are crunchy and sharp, oranges are juicy and sweet.

ACTIVITY 16 (continued)

3 If you found some advantages in Version B you can try to apply the same method to your own essays when comparing two poems.

   a Read two poems you are studying that are about a similar theme or topic.

   b Explore each poem separately, making your own notes or mind maps on each.

   c Brainstorm points of similarity and difference – remember to think about not just *what* the poems are saying, but *how* the poets use language to express their ideas.

   d Finally, use the table below to structure your comparative essay about the poems.

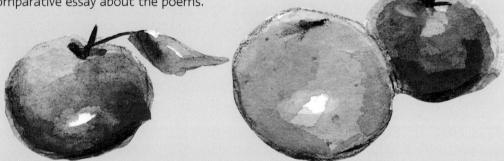

Paragraph summary	Points to write about
Paragraph 1 Summarise briefly what the two poems have in common – and how they differ.	What are the poems about? Do they have a similar topic or theme? Do they both tell a story or describe a place? Do they create a similar mood or atmosphere? In what respects do they differ?
Paragraph 2 Explain the first point in common – ideas or topic covered by each poem?	Develop first similarity – perhaps in the subject matter and the ideas in the poem. Refer to some detail from each poem to back up your point.
Paragraph 3 Explain your second point that the poems have in common.	Develop the similarity – perhaps the form of the poems is similar, or you can see a connection in the use of language, or in the general mood or setting of each poem.
Paragraph 4 Now introduce your first contrast between the poems.	Start by discussing any differences in the main ideas and meanings of both poems. Use phrases such as: *Whereas Poem A is ... On the other hand Poem B is ...*
Paragraph 5 Move on to the next contrast.	Perhaps the two poems differ in their attitude, or mood, or point of view?
Add as many paragraphs as there are significant contrasts to explain.	Remember to keep referring to and quoting from each poem to illustrate your ideas.

How to approach Section A

You will be set one task that requires you to write to explore, imagine or entertain. There will be some guidance on how to approach this task included in the question paper. Although the same task may be set for both tiers, the guidance for the Foundation Tier will be more detailed. The task itself will be clearly defined. Don't write too much; you will have only 45 minutes for planning, writing and checking your work.

Don't make life too complicated

Writing imaginatively under exam conditions is a difficult enough task as it is. Don't make it more stressful than it need be. The task will not necessarily involve writing a story; don't do so unless you are specifically instructed to. You will not have time to write anything too complex or involved and examiners won't expect you to. Keep what you write to something that either is or could be within your own experience. You are in control; the examiner doesn't know you and doesn't know whether what you are writing is true or not – it's up to you and your writing skills to make it convincing.

 REMEMBER

Section A tests your skills in writing to explore, imagine and/or entertain. Although we have looked at these areas separately in this Unit, in the exam question it is possible that they will be combined. What is important is that in your writing you use a suitable register for the task.

How to approach Section B

Shakespeare

In preparation for the examination you will have studied one of the two prescribed Shakespeare plays. As this is an open book exam, you will be allowed to have a copy of the play in the examination room. The tasks set in the examination will require comment, criticism and analysis as appropriate. The topics set for the Foundation Tier are likely to be different from those set for the Higher Tier.

With the thorough knowledge of the play that you have gained from your careful revision, when you open your exam paper all you should have to think about are these questions:

- What does this task actually mean?
- How am I going to use my knowledge of the play to answer it?

Read the task carefully. Don't misread it and assume it is the very one that you were practising the night before when, in fact, the wording is subtly different. Highlight or underline what seem to be the key words in the task.

Poetry selection: *Opening Lines*

The questions on the poems will require comment, criticism and analysis and will be of a similar format no matter whether the poems were written before or after 1914. A typical question will list about four poems from the same section and ask you to write about two of them in order to explain how different poets have treated a similar theme.

Both Foundation and Higher Tier questions will list the same poems and refer to the same topics. However, the wording of the prompts that follow the task will vary, as the language of the Foundation Tier questions will be more straightforward.

 REMEMBER

+ The Anthology is organised thematically so some element of comparison is already present.
+ Keep this overall comparison in mind as the basic structure for your answer.
+ You should draw together points of comparison in your conclusion.
+ Comparing poems also involves writing about points of contrast between them.

Practice paper

UNIT 3/4

SECTION A FOUNDATION AND HIGHER TIER

Writing to explore, imagine, entertain

> 'The child gazed across the darkening landscape; in the distance stood the house, solid and comforting.'

Copy out the sentence above, which is the opening of a story. Then continue the chapter in your own words. You should write about **350–400 words**.

- Do not try to write a complete story, or to explain everything. Concentrate on building up a powerful mood or atmosphere, including some details about the child's feelings.
- Stop writing at the point when the child enters the house.

Plan and check your work carefully.

SECTION B

Texts from the English literary heritage

Answer **two** questions, **one** on Shakespeare and **one** on poetry.

Foundation Tier

1 Shakespeare

Write about some moments in the play you have studied that show important developments in the relationship between two characters. Explain how these examples help your own understanding of the characters involved. Support your answer by careful reference to the play.

2 Poetry: *Opening Lines* (OCR)

Choose from the list below **two** poems that are about the ways in which poets from one age group look at people from a different generation.

How do the poets show their feelings by the words and images they use?

'The Flowers' by Selima Hill
'The Tune the Old Cow Died Of' by Norman Nicholson
'Baby-sitting' by Gillian Clarke
'Imitations' by Dannie Abse

Higher Tier

1 Shakespeare

Explore how the relationship between **two** characters in the play you have studied develops and deepens as the play progresses. Refer in detail to the text in your answer.

2 Poetry: *Opening Lines* (OCR): Section E: 'Generations'

Explore the ways in which people of one generation are described by poets from a different generation, referring closely to the language the poets use.

Choose **two** poems from the list in the Foundation Tier question on poetry.

Reviewing your paper

Section A

Good responses
✔ use correct spelling, punctuation and well-structured paragraphs
✔ show positive merit of vocabulary
✔ use a range of sentence structures
✔ contain interesting and convincing content.

What do you need to do?

Note that the task asks you to concentrate particularly on mood, atmosphere and the child's feelings.

Bring your writing alive! Good imaginative writing includes the use of figures of speech such as *similes* and *metaphors*. Make sure that the ones you use are original and interesting. *Direct speech* is an important feature of narrative writing but don't overdo it. It can lead to problems with punctuation and too much of it can result in a loss of focus and tired vocabulary. Be selective. *Verbs* are important words as they can add dynamic qualities to your writing.

 REMEMBER

✦ It is your responsibility to demonstrate how well you can write. Examiners can only reward what they see. They cannot give you credit for a particular skill unless there is evidence for it – it's up to you to show your qualities.

✦ Good writers don't just choose the first words that come into their heads. They visualise clearly what they are going to describe and then think of the words that will best communicate this to their readers.

✦ Examiners will reward candidates whose writing shows that some positive and conscious decisions have been made about what is being written.

✦ This task tests your competence in writing English; it is not primarily a test of your imaginative or creative faculties – apart from the ways in which you use language.

Question: Why are writing tasks in English GCSE examinations like competitive ice-skating?

Answer: Even in a free programme the ice-skater has to demonstrate the ability to execute certain jumps and movements. Within the freedom of the creative essay, you also have to demonstrate certain linguistic skills and competence.

Section B: Shakespeare

What do you need to do?

Read the question carefully. You will see that both the Foundation and Higher tier questions deal with the same issue but use different vocabulary. The Foundation tier question uses the word 'explain' and the Higher tier question uses the word 'explore'. Keep these words in mind as you write. The questions test your knowledge and understanding (or appreciation) of the play. The key phrases are 'important developments in the relationship between two characters' and 'develops and deepens'. Most probably you will choose the play's two main characters to write about, but you do not have to. Whichever characters you choose, however, you should think about the nature of their relationship. For example, is it one of romantic love, one of dislike or one between two members of a family? Next decide on the main points in that relationship which you are going to describe. It is best to choose only about three or four but the ones you choose show different aspects of the relationship and you should be confident that you can explain these. Now you can begin to write your answer. Remember to describe the moments you have chosen in detail (this shows your knowledge of the play) but also to show your appreciation of it by explaining how you have gained a greater understanding of the characters' overall relationship as a result of what they say and do at these points in the play.

The Globe

 REMEMBER

✦ The examiner has read the play. Your answer should not consist of just re-telling the story!

✦ Focus the points you make clearly on the question you are answering; do not include unnecessary digressions (you only have 30 minutes to answer the question).

✦ Illustrate your points with a quotation and/or reference and then explain how the quotation and the point it illustrates relate to the question you are answering.

✦ The best answers are those that show a clear understanding of how the different aspects of the play contribute to its overall effect and help to further the underlying themes with which the play is concerned.

Section B: Poetry selection: *Opening Lines*

What do you need to do?

As with the questions on the Shakespeare play, you need to show evidence of knowledge and appreciation. The questions on *Opening Lines* require you to write about two poems written on a similar topic. Although the questions do not specifically instruct you to directly compare the two poems, making points of comparison is a good way to show your overall understanding of the ways in which they treat the topic. Choose the two poems in the list with which you are most familiar and which you have most enjoyed. You will have thought about the different ways in which they approach the subject as part of your preparation so you are likely to have some ideas to start with. The task asks you to 'explore' the ways in which the poets describe people. Start with a brief introduction in which you consider in general the poets' attitudes and then comment in detail on the two poems keeping in mind the need to make comparisons between them.

At both tiers the distinguishing feature of the best answers is likely to be the skill with which you write about the poets' use of language. This involves making points about the technical features of the poems such as rhyme, rhythm and the use of poetic devices such as alliteration, similes and metaphor. However, remember that writing about language also involves response to the *words* of the poem and their different associations and ideas, which help to convey the complexity of the poets' thoughts.

Good responses

✔ show a clear understanding of what the poems mean

✔ are aware of the wider issues dealt with by the poets

✔ make focused and helpful comparisons

✔ reveal a perceptive appreciation of the poets' use of language.

A word of warning

Although the ability to use correct technical vocabulary such as *alliteration*, *assonance* and *onomatopoeia* when writing about language will be rewarded by the examiners, do not fall into the trap of thinking that you *must* use this vocabulary.

Writing about poetry is not an exercise in spotting as many technical devices and figures of speech as you can think of.

To say 'The poet has an onomatopoeia in the fifth line but I can't find any alliteration' does not tell the examiner very much about your understanding of the poet's technique. In fact, 'The poet's use of language in the fifth line is very effective in describing the scene as the words he uses suggest the sound of the birds singing' is much more likely to be rewarded despite its lack of technical vocabulary.

Coursework

Instead of opting for the Unit 3/4 examination, you may decide to take the coursework route. The coursework requirements for English are that you should submit for assessment a folder that contains the following *three* items:

✓ one piece of writing to explore, imagine, entertain
✓ one piece of writing about a play by Shakespeare
✓ one piece of writing responding to poetry by a major writer with a well-established critical reputation published either before or after 1914.

Either or both of the reading tasks can be submitted for assessment for English Literature as well, provided that they meet the appropriate criteria.

The decision whether to take the coursework or examination option will be made by you after consultation with your teacher. However, you will certainly do some preparation work in your own time as part of your GCSE course and you may use suitable parts of this for your coursework folder.

Some points to consider

- Your teacher will set and give guidance about suitable coursework tasks but you will be able to modify these to suit your particular ideas.
- For the *writing* task you will be assessed on the *quality* of your writing, not the quantity. You do not have to write at great length. Remember that the equivalent task in the examination requires only a focused piece of descriptive writing.
- Aim to produce a concentrated, well-structured, clearly imagined piece of writing. If you wish, you may produce two shorter, contrasting descriptive passages.
- The *reading* tasks require you to show an understanding of the texts you have studied and an appreciation of the techniques and the language of the writers who produced them.

❗ REMEMBER

- ✦ Coursework allows you the opportunity to produce work in your own time.
- ✦ You are able to spend more time re-drafting your work.
- ✦ Coursework allows you the opportunity to study a Shakespeare play and poems other than those prescribed for the examination set texts.
- ✦ The mark awarded for coursework will be based on the quality of your coursework folder *as a whole*. The maximum total mark for the folder is 40 (20 marks for the writing task and 20 for the two reading tasks together).
- ✦ Coursework must be your own, original work but you are allowed to discuss what you have written with your teacher.
- ✦ If you read books and study aids about the literature you have studied, make sure that you acknowledge them at the end of your essay.

You cannot revise for an English exam in a conventional way; there are very few facts involved for you to cram into your mind the night before an examination. So, how do you prepare for an exam in English? The following may help.

Generally

- ✓ Prepare over a long period of time. Keep focused on what the exam requires throughout the course. Success depends on your approaching the exam in the right frame of mind.
- ✓ Make a point of practising first draft writing during the course. This will help you to avoid making careless mistakes when writing under pressure in the exam.
- ✓ Make sure that you know what the exam involves. Study previous or specimen papers to become familiar with the type of writing you will find in the exam.
- ✓ Become familiar with exam question vocabulary. Make sure that you are not confused when you come across words such as 'explore', 'convey images', 'portray', 'compare', 'contrast'.

Prose selection: *Opening Worlds*

There will be *one* task that will require you to write about *two* of the stories that you have studied. This is an open book exam but you will not be able to take your own copy of the book into the exam with you. Instead you will be provided with a clean copy (that is, one without notes). The following points may help with your revision.

- ✓ Read through each story carefully. Write a brief summary in note form of its main events. Identify what you think are the key stages in the plot.
- ✓ List the main characters in each story. Note their main characteristics and any other important points about them. Support these points with brief quotations or examples from the text.
- ✓ Make similar notes about the setting of each story, again supporting them with quotations or references. Include details of particular aspects of the writer's culture that appear in the story.
- ✓ For each story write down what you consider to be the underlying theme. You can do this in one or two words, e.g. 'education' or 'family relationships'. Think about how this theme is conveyed through the setting, the behaviour of the characters and the language the writer uses.
- ✓ Use the notes you have made to reinforce your reading of the complete stories.
- ✓ All the stories (in shortened form) have appeared in past examination papers from the previous OCR syllabus. Looking at the questions set for earlier exams will help you to identify the issues with which examiners may be concerned.

Shakespeare

- ✓ Read carefully through the play.
- ✓ Concentrate on gaining a confident understanding of the language.
- ✓ Read and make use of the editor's notes and introduction to your edition.
- ✓ Keep pen and paper handy to make notes of important quotations and any thoughts you have about characters' behaviour, etc. as you read through the play.
- ✓ Keep a record of points that you don't really understand and ask your teacher about them during revision sessions.
- ✓ Aim to know the play well enough so that you can see it as a whole and not just as a succession of different scenes.
- ✓ It is best not to try to anticipate specific questions. Instead focus your revision on the following areas, as most questions will involve one or more of them: character, plot, theme, setting, language.

Poetry selection: *Opening Lines*

All questions will allow you to make comparisons. A good way to start your revision is to think of ways in which the poems you have studied can be grouped together. Here are some suggestions.

- ✓ Poems written about similar topics – living creatures, love, mortality, war, etc.
- ✓ Poems written by the same poet.
- ✓ Poems written at about the same period of time – First World War poetry, poems written in the early nineteenth century, etc.
- ✓ Poems that have a specific rhyme scheme or format – sonnets, ballads, free verse, etc.
- ✓ Poems written by women poets.

In the exam

- ✓ Stay calm. Don't rush into writing your answers until you've read the passages and the questions carefully. Underline or highlight key words in the question paper and make notes to help plan your answers.
- ✓ Don't try to write too much for the writing tasks but ensure that what you do write is clear.
- ✓ Leave yourself time to check through what you have written. In particular, watch out for spelling and punctuation mistakes you are prone to make. Remember, it's easier to put in a missing apostrophe than to try to rewrite a whole paragraph!

Skills cross-references and key terms

Speaking and listening

In addition to your reading and writing work, 20% of the marks for English GCSE are awarded for your oral skills. We hope you develop confidence in speaking and listening as you go along.

This assessment will be based on these different situations:

- where it is mainly you doing the talking (e.g. giving a short talk or presentation, or leading a discussion)
- where you take part in some kind of group discussion
- where you take part in a drama-type activity such as a role play.

There are many opportunities for the development and assessment of speaking and listening skills in the activities suggested in this book. You may find the table below useful for reference.

	Extended individual contribution	Group discussion/ interaction	Drama activity
Introduction	Feedback from group discussions e.g. on page 10	Why does English matter, page 5	
Unit 1: Reading non-fiction and media	Feedback from group discussions	Non-fiction or media texts, page 10 Activity 9, page 16 Activity 10, page 20 Activity 11, page 24 Activity 12, page 24 Activity 18, page 34	
Unit 2: Reading different cultures	Feedback from group discussions	Activity 1, page 64 Activity 3, page 65 Activity 7, page 69 Activity 9, page 70 Activity 10, page 71 Activity 14, page 76	
Unit 2: Writing to review/comment/ analyse	Activity 3, page 81 Activity 4, page 82 Activity 8, page 86 Activity 12, page 89	Activity 1, page 79 Activity 3, page 81 Activity 8, page 86 Activity 10, page 87 Activity 12, page 89	
Unit 2: Writing to advise/argue/ persuade	Activity 26, page 104	Activity 15, page 91 Activity 20, page 98 Activity 21, page 99 Activity 22, page 101 Activity 24, page 102	
Unit 3/4: Writing to explore/ imagine/entertain	Feedback from group discussions	Activity 1, page 115 Activity 2, page 116 Activity 5, page 119 Activity 7, page 122	
Unit 3/4: Reading Shakespeare	Feedback from group discussions	Activity 1, page 125 Activity 2, page 127 Activity 3, page 130 Activity 4, page 130 Activity 5, page 131 Activity 6, page 132	Activity 3, page 130 Activity 7, page 134
Unit 3/4: Reading poetry	Activity 11, page 141 Activity 13, page 142 Activity 15, page 146	Activity 8, page 137 Activity 9, page 138	

Developing literacy skills

Throughout your GCSE course it is important that you develop, learn and practise your literacy skills – the quality and accuracy of your use of English is likely to be a major factor in your success in the final examination.

It might be helpful to revise these skills by referring to the relevant sections, listed below, where specific skills are targeted.

Literacy item	Unit 1	Unit 2	Units 3/4
Word level			
Vocabulary	Activity 5, page 14 Activity 12, page 24 Activity 16, page 32 To denote register, page 33 Verbs, tenses, pronouns and connectives, page 43	Adjectives, verbs and adverbs, Activity 11, pages 78 and 79 Connectives, page 98	Activity 12, page 116 Poetic terms and techniques, page 145
Varieties of language		Standard, non-standard and Creole varieties, page 78	
Punctuation		Punctuation of speech, page 78	
Sentence level	Activity 18, page 34 First/third person narrative, page 68	Expressing opinions, page 83 Expressing agreement, disagreement and doubt, page 87 Expressing analysis and suggesting solutions, page 90 Connecting arguments, page 98	Reported speech, page 121 First/third person narrative, page 123 Activity 10, page 140 Poetic terms and techniques, page 145
		Similes and metaphors, and Activity 13, page 75 Persuasive techniques, pages 103 and 104 Activity 26, page 104	
Grammar		Impersonal register, page 98	
Whole text level	Activity 5, page 40		Verse and prose, page 133
Using quotations		Writing about the texts, page 77	
Paragraphs		Commenting, page 87 Connecting paragraphs and sentences, page 98	
Structure	Section A Question 2, page 55	Activity 9, page 86: Smacking Persuasive techniques, pages 103 and 104 Activity 26, page 104	Poetic terms and techniques, page 145

Key terms (glossary)

Accent: the distinctive way in which people pronounce their words

Adjective: class of word that gives information/ description about nouns (*blue, hot, easy*)

Adverb: class of word that tells us how, where or when an action occurs (*slowly, here, yesterday*)

Advise: to offer guidance and/or instructions to your readers

Alliteration: repetition of similar consonant sounds at the beginning of words for effect

Analyse: to explain in detail what has caused a situation or event, or to point out the methods used in a piece of writing

Argue: to offer a series of reasons that lead to conclusion or point of view

Assonance: repetition of similar vowel sounds, but which do not actually rhyme

Ballad: a traditional kind of poem that tells a story

Caesura: a break or pause in the middle of a stanza or line, usually shown by punctuation

Cliché: an often-used and predictable expression

Collate: to bring together information on the same topic from two or more different sources

Colloquial: a very informal style of language

Comment: to offer a personal opinion of or response to a topic or piece of writing

Connectives: word and phrases, such as *because, and, after*, etc., that join phrases and sentences together

Creole: a variety of language that is the result of two languages influencing each other, e.g. Caribbean Creole reflects both English and African linguistic influence

Criterion (sing.) /**criteria** (pl.): standards or qualities by which something or someone is deemed to be good, effective or successful

Culture: the distinctive life-style, values and belief of a community

Describe: to create for readers a vivid impression of something or someone

Dialect: the words and expressions that are typical of a particular regional variety of English

Direct speech: where the actual words spoken by characters are quoted directly in a story, usually using **speech marks** ('   ')

Emotive: language designed to create an emotional reaction

Enjambement: where the sense (and sentence) runs on from line to line

Explain: to make something clear and help readers understand an idea or process

Evaluate: to make a judgement about the merits of someone or something

Fiction (see also **non-fiction**): writing that is invented or imagined

First person: the point of view of 'I' or 'we', sometimes used to narrate stories

Genre: a recognisable type of book or film

Iambic pentameter: a line of verse that has five stressed syllables alternating with five unstressed

Imperative: a direct command, such as 'Go away!'

Inform: to convey factual information

Metaphor: an implied comparison between two things or ideas

Non-fiction (see also **fiction**, above): writing that is based on real-life situations or facts

Noun: class of words that name people, things or ideas (*engineer, table, happiness*)

Objective view (see also **subjective** view): an assessment that is not just a personal opinion and tries to take a neutral or detached viewpoint

Onomatopoeia: use of words with sounds that resemble the noises they describe

Parallelism: repetition of the same phrase or sentence structure

Presentational devices: the various visual methods used to make a text appear interesting and attractive

Personification: a kind of metaphor that refers to objects as if they were human

Persuade: to seek to influence the thoughts feelings or actions of an audience

Pronoun: a class of words which refer to people and things, such as *I, me, you, he, she, it, they*

Quatrain: a set of four lines within a poem

Register: the distinctive style or tone of a text (e.g. whether it is formal or informal)

Reported speech: where the speech of characters is not quoted directly but related by the narrator/storyteller (*He said that he was going to …*)

Review: to consider the positive and negative aspects of an event or experience

Rhetoric: a range of techniques used to create effective or persuasive language

Rhyming couplet: a pair of successive lines that rhyme

Simile: a comparison made by using 'like' or 'as'

Sonnet: a poem with 14 lines and a regular pattern of rhyme and rhythm

Stanza: a verse of a poem

Subjective view (see also **objective** view, above): a viewpoint based strongly on a personal opinion or feeling

Third person: the point of view used when a story is told by a narrator who is not a character in the story and who refers to characters as *he, she* or *they*

Verb: class of words that usually refer to actions (*walk, eat, destroy*)